1395

D0624401

HALLE
BERRY

DISCARDED
Richmond Public Library

BELOW: Halle Berry at a New York screening of *Monster's Ball* in December 2001.

HALLE BERRY

DANIEL O'BRIEN

REYNOLDS & HEARN LTD
LONDON

31143007024111
B BERRY, H.
O'Brien, Daniel.
Halle Berry

Cover and interior images
© Rex Features

First published in 2003 by
Reynolds & Hearn Ltd
61a Priory Road
Kew Gardens
Richmond
Surrey TW9 3DH

© Daniel O'Brien 2003

All rights reserved. No part of this
publication may be reproduced, in
any form or by any means, without
permission from the publisher.

A CIP catalogue record for this book
is available from the British Library.

ISBN 1 903111 38 2

Designed by James King.

Printed and bound in Malta
by Interprint Ltd.

ACKNOWLEDGEMENTS

My thanks to Marcus Hearn, David
O'Leary, David Pratt, Richard Reynolds,
Jonathan Rigby and Beth Richards.
Special thanks to Gary Kramer, who
conducted in-depth research into the
Halle Berry movies *Strictly Business*,
Boomerang, *Father Hood*, *Losing Isaiah*
and *Rich Man's Wife*, above and beyond
the call of duty.

CONTENTS

INTRODUCTION

HOLLYWOOD actress Halle Berry has her own official website, 'Hallewood', which is a treat for lovers of celebrity kitsch. Eager net-surfers are greeted by an animated cartoon version of Berry, flanked by her two Maltese dogs, Polly and Willy. The graphic style is curiously reminiscent of the title sequence for *Bewitched* (1964-71), the twee supernatural sitcom starring the late Elizabeth Montgomery. The cartoon Berry stands on a purple road, lined with giant-sized make-up items and stationery. Dressed in flared grey slacks and a midriff-baring mauve top, Halle Berrytoon looks cool, friendly and definitely non-threatening. The site features beauty tips, choice recipes and even a glimpse of Berry's personal wardrobe.

What 'Hallewood' doesn't offer is any great insight into how a troubled mixed-race woman from Cleveland, Ohio, became the first black star to win the Best Actress Academy Award. The former model and soap opera star who feared she'd never be accepted as a 'real' actress is now on Hollywood's red-hot list. Having survived a tough childhood, Halle Berry endured abusive relationships, a failed marriage, a rumoured suicide attempt and years of ingrained racism. This is not the kind of background normally associated with a spokeswoman for Revlon cosmetics.

Berry's uneven film career moved in fits and starts for nearly a decade before she really made it. Up until her Oscar triumph in *Monster's Ball* (2001), Halle Berry was probably best known for flashing her breasts in the daft action movie *Swordfish* (2001). Two years earlier, she'd given an award-winning performance in the television drama *Introducing Dorothy Dandridge* (1999). Respected stars don't usually lounge on sun beds in their bikini bottoms. Not even for $500,000.

The history of African-American stars in Hollywood goes back a mere five decades. Forty years after *Darktown Jubilee* (1914), supposedly the first all-black film., Sidney Poitier became established during the 1950s. Poitier remained Hollywood's only black leading man for nearly two decades. Former football player Jim Brown played co-starring roles in the 1960s, but found his career drifting until the rise of 1970s blaxploitation, which conferred transient stardom on Richard Roundtree and Fred Williamson. During the late 1970s and 1980s, comedians Richard Pryor and Eddie Murphy both found success in Hollywood. A few years later, more heavyweight black actors such as Denzel Washington, Danny Glover, Morgan Freeman, Wesley Snipes, Samuel L Jackson and Will Smith became big names. The broad comedy end of the market was catered to by the Wayans bothers, led by Keenan Ivory and Damon.

To this day, black actresses suffer from a two-fold prejudice in Hollywood, and few have become big names. Led by actress-singer Dorothy Dandridge, one of Halle Berry's inspirations, a handful experienced fleeting stardom, including Pam Grier, pop diva Diana Ross and comedienne Whoopi Goldberg. None of them have enjoyed lasting success in the movies. More recently, Whitney Houston, Angela Bassett and Vanessa Williams have all played leading roles, yet they rarely compete on level terms with white stars.

Halle Berry is Hollywood's favourite kind of 'black' actress: tall, slim, light-skinned and attractive in a Caucasian rather than a Negroid fashion. Studio executives are comfortable pairing Berry with older white males, whether Kyle MacLachlan (*The Flintstones*), Warren Beatty (*Bulworth*), John Travolta (*Swordfish*), Billy Bob Thornton (*Monster's Ball*) or Pierce Brosnan (*Die Another Day*). Confident of her appearance, Berry is well aware that it can be held against her:

Sometimes you take advantage of your looks, other times you put them behind you. It's something I've battled against. People think if you look this way you can't play downtrodden.

An accomplished actress, Berry has shown a flair for both comedy and drama, often battling poor-quality scripts. Her big screen debut in *Jungle Fever* (1991), as a drug-addicted prostitute, revealed a strong, committed film talent. Berry has a reputation for being both good-natured and honourable, qualities not always found in the movie business. Even hardened showbiz journalists find her utterly charming in person. That said, Berry has no time for the tabloid press ("I don't dignify those rags with a response"), and successfully sued one paper for printing a story about her stepdaughter.

In terms of star pampering, incidentally, Berry's demands are modest. She is a big fan of manicures, pedicures, massages, body scrubs and rubdowns, not to mention a skin treatment called 'Cleopatra's Milk',

which involves huge quantities of warm, thick cow juice. Interested parties should check out the Grand Wailea, on the Hawaiian island of Maui. When it comes to food, "…nothing is better than a big bowl of spaghetti carbonara", though grilled tuna with garlic mashed potatoes and butter pecan ice cream come close.

After years of steady work in Hollywood, Halle Berry seemed stuck in a rut. Her supporting role in the Eddie Murphy hit *Boomerang* (1992) did not lead to great film offers. Following *The Flintstones* (1994), a calculated career move, Berry won starring roles in *Losing Isaiah* (1995), *Race the Sun* (1996), *The Rich Man's Wife* (1996) and *B*A*P*S* (1997), all of which flopped at the American box-office. Berry hoped that the interracial adoption drama *Losing Isaiah* would make her name as both a dramatic actress and a rising star, yet the film proved disappointing.

In 1997, the Acapulco Black Film Festival handed Halle Berry a Career Achievement Award. Coming in the year of *B*A*P*S*, one of Berry's worst movies, this could be seen as misjudged, not to say premature. Active in feature films for only six years, Berry had few major credits to her name. That said, as a black actress regularly employed by Hollywood in starring or co-starring roles, Halle Berry had already beaten the odds.

Berry's biggest commercial successes include three movies for producer Joel Silver, a specialist in high-concept thrillers who comes calling every five years. While *The Last Boy Scout* (1991), *Executive Decision* (1996) and *Swordfish* (2001) are hot on wisecracks, male bonding and heavy-duty action sequences, they do not offer good roles for women. Variously cast as a stripper, a flight attendant and a *femme fatale* counter-terrorist, Berry often looks surplus to requirements in these films.

Attempting to balance commercial movies with more serious films, Berry has also tried to alternate between strong, non-stereotyped black characters and parts not specifically written for an African-American. Up until *Monster's Ball*, Berry's strongest dramatic roles were in *Bulworth* and the TV movie *Introducing Dorothy Dandridge*. Several of her feature films have gone straight to video in Britain, hardly the most encouraging sign for a budding star.

While *Monster's Ball* has raised Halle Berry's career to a new level, it remains to be seen if she translates this success into full-fledged stardom. Berry sounds confident, telling *Guardian* journalist Libby Brooks: "…now I'm really at the party, and I'm getting opportunities that I never had before." As a black woman in a business controlled by white males, Halle Berry has no illusions that Hollywood will change overnight. While the prejudices remain, however, the victories will be all the sweeter. Interviewed by Brooks, Berry made her feelings clear:

> …when you can achieve what you set out to with those things stacked against you, the amount of confidence and self-validation that you are then rewarded with makes it so worth it.

Realistic about the movie business, Halle Berry looks to audiences as much as studio executives for her opportunities as a leading black actress, telling Bruce Kirkland:

> It's all about money in Hollywood and that's why I can't take it all that personally…When we start making movies that show black people in a positive way, and people come out to support them, when those films make money, I'll have all the chances in the world.

PUSHING IT

HALLE Maria Berry was born on 14 August 1968 in Cleveland, Ohio. Her African-American father, Jerome, was a former hospital attendant, then employed as a janitor. Her white English mother, Judith, worked as a psychiatric nurse. Born in Liverpool, Judith met Jerome Berry while he was serving in the United States Army. They already had one daughter, Heidi, born in 1964. Jerome and Judith Berry named their second child after the historic Halle Building, in downtown Cleveland. This local landmark, now filled with offices, took its name from the long-gone Halle Brothers department store.

Things were not good in the Berry household. A violent alcoholic, Jerome frequently attacked Judith, occasionally turning on Halle's older sister Heidi. Halle Berry's first memory is of violence: "It's sad but true." Jerome's heavy-drinking also hurt the family financially. In 1972, when Halle was just four years old, Jerome walked out on his family, he and Judith divorcing. While Judith and her daughters continued to suffer financial hardship, their lives improved immeasurably.

As the white single mother of two black children, Judith Berry faced prejudice from both sides of the racial divide. Living in the predominantly white suburbs of Bedford and Oakwood Village, she encountered people who couldn't accept that a blonde, blue-eyed Caucasian had given birth to non-white daughters. The young Halle Berry soon picked up on this, as she explained to journalist Robin Taylor:

It's been my way of life since I can remember. Especially being the product of a white mother and black father – I dealt with it a lot and watched my mother deal with it.

Six years later, Jerome Berry reappeared on the scene, asking Judith to forgive him. Hoping to bring the family back together, Halle's mother agreed to give her ex-husband another chance. Now ten, Halle Berry endured what she later described as "…the worst year of my life". Having seen nothing of Jerome since she was a small girl, Halle had her life turned upside down by his traumatic return. Unwilling, or unable, to abandon his old ways, Jerome quickly reverted to violent behaviour, drinking heavily and lashing out at Judith and Heidi. While he never abused Halle physically, she found the emotional torment almost unbearable. One evening, while the family were seated at the dinner table, Jerome grew irritated with their pet dog, a toy Maltese, and threw the animal across the room. After 12 hellish months, Jerome abandoned his wife and daughters for good.

To this day, Halle Berry has never forgiven her father, attributing many of her personal problems to his behaviour. Berry remains extremely close to her mother, Judith, though her relationship with sister Heidi is said to be distant. She also has two half-sisters, Yolanda and Renee, and a half brother, Anthony, from Jerome Berry's first marriage. Like Heidi, they have little contact with her.

While Jerome Berry had finally disappeared from her life, Halle still faced a daily battle with racial played Trish Carlin, the maternal, strictly above-board head of a modelling agency for teenagers (hence the title). Cast as young hopeful Emily Franklin, the equally ambitious Halle Berry had little to do but look good on camera. Nevertheless, she made the most of this limited opportunity, determined to prove herself.

Adopting a 'method' approach to acting, Berry liked to stay in character between takes, which puzzled some of her fellow cast members. Interviewed by *Calgary Sun* reporter Tyler McLeod in 1998, Berry still sounded very serious about her craft: "As an actor, in order to get certain emotions and express certain feelings, you always have to draw on your own experience if you're going to make it real."

No longer a teenager herself, Halle Berry found life as a 'living doll' less than stimulating after the first few weeks. On the bright side, the show offered regular, well-paid, high-profile work and could get her noticed. As Berry put it: "…I got my first TV show and got paid more money than I'd ever gotten in my life …I was, y'know, 'I think I can do this'."

Living Dolls received its US network premiere on 26 September 1989. Hoping to repeat the success of *Who's the Boss?*, Warner Bros and ABC soon realised that they'd bet on the wrong comic situation. As Tony Danza carried on strong for another three years, *Living Dolls* died during its first season.

Berry's acting career had got off to a reasonable, if modest start. While *Living Dolls* suffered an abrupt cancellation, further offers of television work were coming in. Berry's personal life was not in such good shape. She seemed to have found true love early on, falling for a fellow actor. Unfortunately, he turned out to be as violent as Berry's

father, beating her up at least once. During the attack, Berry suffered a ruptured left eardrum, which caused permanent hearing damage. To this day, Berry is largely deaf in her left ear and requires a hearing aid. With typical honesty, Berry admits that she is too vain to wear the device in public. While the identity of Berry's attacker has not been made public, he's rumoured to be a well-known Hollywood figure.

Already suffering from diabetes, Berry bore her new disability with remarkable stoicism. Diagnosed as diabetic in 1989, Berry has never let the condition interfere with her work, injecting herself with insulin during breaks: "Sometimes, in the middle of a work day, it can be a little inconvenient to say: I have to go shoot up. Can you excuse me please?" According to Berry, she suffered through several more volatile relationships. When the abuse from one boyfriend became physical she fought back, then walked out.

Berry's subsequent television work included *They Came from Outer Space* (1990), playing Rene in the episode 'Hair Today, Gone Tomorrow'. She also appeared in *Amen*, cast as Claire in the

RIGHT: *Knots Landing*. Cast as Debbie Porter, Halle goes for the clinch with co-star Larry Riley.

13

episode 'Unforgettable', first shown on 19 January 1991. Less than a month later, Berry could be seen in *A Different World*, playing Jaclyn in the St. Valentine's special 'Love, Hillman-Style', broadcast on 14 February. The same year, Berry won a co-starring role in the popular soap opera *Knots Landing*. This *Dallas* spin-off had been running since 1979, emerging from the shadow of its better-known cousin. Signing up for the 1991-92 season, Berry played Debbie Porter.

Away from the worlds of soap and sitcom, Berry supplemented her income appearing in a pop promo. Producer-performer R Kelly and Public Announcement needed a leading lady for their 1991 'Honey Love' video. Obviously short on inspiration, Kelly wanted to re-enact a scene from the raunchy *9? Weeks* (1986). Called upon to smoulder around Kelly, Berry did her job with commendable professionalism.

Around this time, Berry began dating actor Wesley Snipes, who looked set to become a big name in Hollywood. Snipes' film career to date included several broad comedies, notably *Wild Cats* (1986) with Goldie Hawn, *Critical Condition* (1987) starring comedian Richard Pryor, and *Major League* (1989) with Charlie Sheen. Snipes had also appeared in the much darker *King of New York* (1990), directed by Abel Ferrara, and Spike Lee's *Mo' Better Blues* (1990), starring Denzel Washington

At the time, Shelton Jackson 'Spike' Lee was America's leading black filmmaker, known for provocative, race-themed movies such as *She's Gotta Have It* (1986) and *Do the Right Thing* (1989). Impressed with Snipes' work on *Mo' Better Blues*, Lee offered him the starring role in *Jungle Fever* (1991). A co-production between Hollywood major Universal and Lee's own Forty Acres and A Mule Filmworks, this $14 million movie dealt with the provocative theme of interracial romance.

It's possible that Berry's relationship with Snipes helped secure her a small role in *Jungle Fever*. That said, Spike Lee is not the kind of director who panders to his actors' whims. While Snipes probably brought Berry to Lee's attention, she got the part on her own merits, cast as a crack cocaine addict offering discount blowjobs. Berry prepared for her big screen debut by going unwashed for several days prior to shooting. Presumably the cast and crew didn't object.

Like much of Spike Lee's work, *Jungle Fever* is an ambitious, uneven film, playing with too many ideas in the course of its sprawling narrative. Snipes stars as Flipper Purify, an affluent, happily married family man with a nice apartment in Harlem. A successful architect, Purify feels undervalued at work, eventually quitting to set up on his own. Showing early signs of mid-life crisis, or just being a jerk, he begins an affair with his Italian-American secretary, Angie (Annabella Sciorra).

Whatever its faults, *Jungle Fever* boasts an impressive supporting cast. Tim Robbins and Brad Dourif appear as Flipper's smug, outwardly liberal employers, who have no intention of making him an equal partner in the firm. Spike Lee isn't big on subtlety. As an actor, Lee plays his customary role of the hero's best friend, who lends a sympathetic ear then tells all to his wife.

Jungle Fever's interracial affair is supplemented with a heavy duty subplot involving drug addiction. Samuel L Jackson, who'd appeared in *Do the Right Thing*, plays Flipper's dissolute brother Gator, a crack cocaine addict A former crack user himself, Jackson had only recently beaten his addiction when *Jungle Fever* went into

RIGHT:
June 2002: Halle Berry with Spike Lee at the Directors Guild Awards. Spike directed Halle in *Jungle Fever*.

ABOVE:
Jungle Fever. Halle Berry rehearses with Wesley Snipes and Annabella Sciorra, under the watchful eye of director Spike Lee.

production. Cutting a distinctive figure with his scruffy beard, baseball cap, dungarees, anorak and crucifix necklace, Gator knocks back the booze and candy bars. Also sporting a soiled jogging outfit, this amoral addict lies, begs, cheats and steals, scrounging $100 and $50 'loans' off his kind-hearted mother and the less sympathetic Flipper.

Halle Berry plays Vivian, Gator's aggressive yet pathetic junkie girlfriend. While Berry has far less screen time than Samuel L Jackson, she makes a fair impression. Berry had no first hand experience of crack-cocaine, relying on research and her own intuition. The most memorable supporting character is a street whore, desperate for drug money. Accosting Flipper on the street, she offers him bargain oral sex, in front of his small daughter: "Five dollars, daddy, I'll suck your dick." When Flipper refuses, she drops the price to three dollars. Clearly disturbed by this encounter, Flipper angrily grabs his uncomprehending child: "If I ever see you using drugs, I'll kill you."

In the film's last scene, Flipper runs into the prostitute again. Times are obviously bad, as her asking price for fellatio has dropped even further: "Yo, daddy, I'll suck your big black dick for two dollars." In an unexpected gesture, Flipper clutches the young woman to him with a cry of "Nooooooo!", as the camera swoops down from a high angle to frame Flipper's anguished face. It's a memorable, if heavy-handed finale, endorsing Spike Lee's basic point. Crack-cocaine is an epidemic, destroying individuals, families and the entire population. If the black community is to survive, it must reclaim the junkies as its own people rather than marginalise and demonise them.

Overall, *Jungle Fever* is a very misanthropic polemic, arguing that harmony between New York's various ethnic groups is nothing more than a pipe dream. The racial hatred expressed by the people around Flipper, whether WASPs, Italian-Americans or African-Americans, is insurmountable. Though well-handled, the drug subplot feels tacked on to the central interracial affair, breaking the movie in half. And, under the circumstances, Stevie Wonder's jaunty title song seems inappropriate.

Opening in the United States on 7 June 1991, *Jungle Fever* stirred up the controversy expected of a Spike Lee 'joint'. While stars Wesley Snipes and Samuel L Jackson got most of the press attention, Halle Berry's solid contribution did not go unnoticed. The film grossed a respectable $32.48 million at the North American box-office.

Berry had more screen time in her second movie, *Strictly Business* (1991). This modest romantic comedy was intended to showcase the talents of budding black stars Tommy Davidson and Joseph C. Phillips. The fact that neither Davidson nor Phillips are household names a decade on says something about its success. Davidson had achieved a measure of fame on the television comedy show *In Living Color* (1990), which also launched the Wayans brothers. Co-star Berry received a special credit: 'And Halle Berry as Natalie', a mixed blessing under the circumstances. *Strictly Business* was directed by television graduate Kevin Hooks, with some uncredited assistance from Rolando Hudson. The son of respected black actor Robert Hooks, Hooks Jr's small-screen credits included *Roots: The Gift* (1988), the third, and least, instalment in the epic saga of defiant plantation slave Kunta Kinte.

In terms of story, *Strictly Business* is strictly to formula. Waymon Tinsdale III

flippant and deadly serious. High-quality car explosions blend with vicious bouts of violence, as Joe and Jimmy battle an illegal gambling syndicate headed by football team owner Sheldon Marcone (Noble Willingham). The seriously nasty bad guys are well cast, one repellent specimen meeting a messy rotor-blade death.

The token female characters are depicted with extreme male chauvinism. Sarah Hallenbeck (Field) justifies her affair on the grounds that Joe has lost his pride and self-respect. And she's lonely. Joe's daughter, Darian (Danielle Harris), has a sharp tongue and foul mouth, yet helps save her father's life in a tight spot.

An exotic dancer who also waits tables, Cory (Berry) claims to have a stalker. Attempting to interest Hallenbeck in the case, a sleazy fellow private eye gives her the thumbs up: "She's hot, Joe. She rates a three on my finger scale." (Don't ask.) Cory makes her entrance in a skimpy black top and a very short, very tight red skirt. Her dancing outfit consists of a blonde wig, cowboy hat, piebald chaps and a sheriff's badge over each nipple. Waving a pistol in suggestive fashion, Cory gyrates to the strains of 'Ridin' on the Range', slithering around a pole and grasping her butt-cheeks. Still, there's no actual nudity. Berry would adopt the blonde look again in B*A*P*S and X-Men.

Unfortunately for her, Cory hasn't been honest about the 'stalker' problem. It seems she's been blackmailing Sheldon Marcone, a former lover. Looking to get Jimmy his old job back, Cory tries to play the powerful, ruthless Marcone at his own game. Big mistake. Back-ended in her car, Cory is machine-gunned by hitmen. Dressed in a tasseled white jacket, Cory performs a slow-motion bonnet tumble before hitting the ground,

extremely lifeless. Written out of the film within the first 30 minutes, Berry at least plays dead with conviction, the camera lingering on her prone, bloody corpse. Berry's last line, "Can't you fuckin' drive?", proved oddly prophetic. Ten years on, the tabloid press would ask her the same question.

Gone, but not forgotten, the deceased Cory gives Jimmy a personal reason to hunt down the villains. A middle-aged Good Ole Boy from the Deep South, Sheldon Marcone has no respect for the dead woman: "She's one of the sweetest little whores I ever tasted." Already wracked with guilt for having cheated on Cory, Jimmy won't take this kind of talk. Money aside, it's not clear what Cory saw in Marcone, who makes *Monster's Ball* patriarch Buck Grotowski look almost pleasant. Incidentally, Cory dies without knowing that Jimmy was unfaithful. While Joe and Sarah Hallenbeck seem reconciled by the fadeout, Jimmy will never know what might have been, good or bad.

Opening in the United States on 13 December 1991, *The Last Boy Scout* offered audiences some high-class Yuletide carnage. The film grossed nearly $60 million in North America alone, suggesting that Willis could still cut it as an action hero.

Having proved her worth as a prostitute, dancer and stripper, Berry finally got a desk job in *Boomerang* (1992). Produced by Paramount, this romantic comedy starred Eddie Murphy, whose once high-flying career had lost a lot of altitude. While Murphy supplied the 'original' story for *Boomerang*, Paramount left the screenplay in other hands and, looking to put their prize asset back on top, budgeted the film at a tidy $42 million. If this seems a lot for a character-driven comedy, it should be remembered that Murphy had grown

RIGHT:
Boomerang. Halle with Eddie Murphy, her leading man and one-time lover.

accustomed to the best of everything.

Murphy plays Marcus Graham, a womanising executive who gets a taste of his own medicine when he falls for new boss Jacqueline Broyer, an early

starring role for Robin Givens. Having burned up the male cast in *A Rage in Harlem* (1991), Givens seemed ideal casting as the woman Murphy can't control.

The director, Reginald Hudlin, had

scored a hit with hip-hop comedy *House Party* (1990), which he also scripted. The latter was produced by his brother, Warrington Hudlin, who also came on board for *Boomerang*. The Hudlins assembled an impressive if eclectic collection of African-American talent, including singers Grace Jones and Eartha Kitt, pioneering black filmmaker Melvin Van Peebles, *Saturday Night Live* comic Chris Rock and future star Martin Lawrence. The supporting cast also included actor-choreographer Geoffrey Holder, best known for his spooky turn as Baron Samedi in the Roger Moore's first James Bond film, *Live and Let Die* (1973). For her part, Grace Jones had turned up 12 years in Moore's last , *A View to a Kill* (1985). Another 17 years on, Halle Berry would make her own contribution to the long-running Bond franchise.

Set against the backdrop of the cosmetics industry, *Boomerang* is patchy, to say the least. Working as a mere hired hand, Hudlin can do little with the inferior script. While there are some big laughs, the overall movie is crude, sparsely plotted and ridiculously overstretched at nearly two hours. Much of the screenplay seems designed to stroke Murphy's ego, praising his arse, for instance, as the world's finest. Best known for her stormy marriage to boxer Mike Tyson, Robin Givens acts Murphy off the screen at times as his predatory, hard-as-nails boss. Cast as 'Strange', Grace Jones overacts wildly. That said, Strange at least has a spectacular entrance, arriving at a chic party via a helicopter and chariot.

Berry is the entirely respectable Angela Lewis, a graphic designer who meets Marcus at a party. Cast as the 'girl next door' to Givens' queen bitch, Berry gives a decent, star-calibre performance. Angela is initially more interested in Marcus' best friend, Gerard, played by *In Living Color* actor David Alan Grier. Insecure and indecisive, Gerard seems out of his depth with the more confident Angela. Their good night kiss after a date is almost touching. Closing his eyes, Gerard misses Angela's lips, meeting her forehead instead. A cultured woman, Angela speaks Korean, though not very well. Once Jacqueline has dumped Marcus, he and Angela become close. They bond over *Star Trek* and realise that their feelings run deeper than friendship. Still hung up on Jacqueline, Marcus vacillates between the two women before finally choosing Angela.

Berry gets her best scene when Angela turns on Marcus, letting him know how much he's hurt her feelings. By the end of the film, Angela has become a tough corporate businesswoman, which seems to be down to love. Contending with a weak script, Berry shows her potential as a leading lady. Berry certainly holds her own against the self-satisfied Murphy, with whom she had a brief offscreen relationship.

Released in the United States on 1 July 1992, *Boomerang* didn't open in Britain until 30 October. Paramount's hefty investment in Eddie Murphy's magic touch paid off, the film taking $131 million worldwide. The critics were generally unimpressed, though *Time Out* reviewer Steve Grant saw the positive side: "…it's good to see a black-based film *not* concerned with guns, drugs and dem dere pigs". Halle Berry picked up two MTV Movie Award nominations, for Best Breakthrough Performance and Most Desirable Female. While not quite in the Academy Award class, this marked a step up from being a Living Doll.

LIVING IN THE PAST

ABOVE: Toiling in the fields in *Queen*.

WITH four feature films to her name, including a couple of blockbusters, Halle Berry had made a good start in the movies. That said, she was still a supporting player, whose star quality had not been rewarded with star status. Since *Jungle Fever*, her roles had been largely decorative, making few demands on her acting talent. When television came calling with a dramatic leading role, Berry jumped at the chance.

Putting her big screen career on hold, Berry agreed to play the title role in *Queen* (1993), cast as a former slave who witnesses the fall of the Old South. Produced by the CBS network, this lavish mini-series was based on a story by celebrated black author Alex Haley (1921-92), best known for *Roots* (1976), the 'factional' story of enslaved African Kunta Kinte. Carefully tailored to both a black and white readership, *Roots* chronicled the grim history of African Americans, leavening the unsavoury details with a sense of optimism. A huge commercial and critical success, *Roots* won the Pulitzer Prize for literature.

The 1977 television adaptation met with similar acclaim, watched by 50 per cent of America's entire TV audience. A landmark in the history of small screen drama, the TV *Roots* was directed by John Erman, who also helmed the first sequel, *Roots: The Next Generation* (1979). Significantly, Erman passed on *Roots: The Gift* (1988), leaving the way clear for Kevin Hooks. Looking to repeat the success of the first *Roots* television series, CBS hired John Erman to direct *Queen*.

Sadly, Alex Haley died during preproduction on *Queen*. The task of turning Haley's story into a workable script passed to screenwriter David Stevens, whose film credits included the hit Australian movie *Breaker Morant* (1980). The cast included some of Hollywood finest black actors, notably Danny Glover, Dennis Haysbert, Paul Winfield, Ossie Davis and Lonette McKee. Davis and McKee had both worked on Spike Lee's *Jungle Fever*, though not in scenes with Halle Berry. *Queen* also featured cameos from respected stars Martin Sheen and Ann-Margret; the latter had worked with Erman on four previous television dramas, including an acclaimed 1984 version of Tennessee Williams' *A Streetcar Named Desire*. Most of the exteriors for *Queen* were shot on authentic locations in Charleston, South Carolina.

Queen is based on the life of Alex Haley's paternal grandmother. The story takes in slavery, the American Civil War (1861-65), the emancipation of black slaves and the troubled post-war period of reconstruction. The mixed-race daughter of a slave and a plantation owner, Queen faces prejudice from both sides as she struggles to make her way through traumatic times.

Having contended with the same double-edged racism all her life, Halle Berry brings an extra level of conviction to an impressive, impassioned performance. Ageing several decades over the course of the narrative, Berry is convincing as an old lady, helped by some decent make-up. As Deep South plantation melodramas go, *Queen* is pretty good, helped by strong production values, assured direction and fine performances. The familiar story elements are generally well-handled. Some Halle Berry fans believe that *Queen* remains her best role, surpassing even *Monster's Ball*. CBS premiered *Queen* on 14 February 1993.

Berry then made a brief return trip to Universal for the gangsta rap spoof *CB4* (1993), a vehicle for rising comedy star Chris Rock. One of the few bright spots in *Boomerang*, Rock would soon become a serious rival to Eddie Murphy. The film was produced and co-scripted by Nelson George, who'd worked on screenplay for *Strictly Business*. *CB4* is also notable for employing a female director, Tamra Davis, one of the very few active in Hollywood. Davis had recently achieved a cult hit with *Guncrazy* (1992), proving she could handle 'macho' material. This effective white-trash-love-on-the-run drama had also suggested that former child star Drew Barrymore was on the comeback trail.

CB4 follows the adventures of California rappers Cell Block 4: Stab Master Arson, Mad Mike and MC Gusto. The big joke is that these dangerous muthas are in fact nice, clean-living, middle-class boys. That said, the trio certainly know how to pile on the macho bullshit. While hardly rap's answer to *This Is Spinal Tap* (1983), still the benchmark for spoof 'rockumentaries', *CB4* has its moments, many of them gross. The script, written by Chris Rock with Nelson George, is often amusing and well-observed,

LEFT: Halle with fellow cast members Jasmine Guy and Timothy Daley in *Queen*.

BELOW: *Queen* comes to terms with motherhood.

though many of the jokes will be lost on non-fans. As MC Gusto, aka Albert, Rock demonstrates his comic gifts and obvious star quality.

Berry puts in an appearance as herself, along with Isaac Hayes, Ice T, Ice Cube, Flavour Flav and Eazy E. The supporting cast also includes Charlie Murphy, Eddie's brother, and the late Phil Hartman, a regular guest voice on *The Simpsons*. *CB4*'s hip hop numbers are supplemented by the more authentic gangsta sound of Public Enemy, Beastie Boys, PM Dawn and MC Ren. Released in the United States on 12 March 1993, *CB4* grossed a modest $17.953 million at the box-office.

By the mid-1990s, Halle Berry was working regularly in the movies, with the occasional leading role on television. Though by no means a star, she had already achieved a level of success denied the vast majority of actors, black or white. Away from the camera, Berry appeared to have found some stability in her troubled private life. Aside from Wesley Snipes and Eddie Murphy, her boyfriends supposedly included soap opera actor Shemar Moore and star basketball player Shaquille O'Neal. While these relationships came and went, Berry began a serious romance with another leading sportsman, David Justice, a baseball player for the Atlanta Braves. On New Year's Eve 1992, she and Justice were married in a private ceremony held at his Atlanta home. Accepting that Justice could not relocate to Los Angeles, Berry commuted between the two cities.

Continuing her screen career, Berry gained second billing, if little else, on *Father Hood* (1993), a dismal action comedy that stints on both items. Produced by Hollywood Pictures in association with Disney distributor Buena Vista, the film marked Patrick Swayze's fall from stardom. Six years earlier, Swayze burned up the screen in *Dirty Dancing* (1987), following this smash hit with the camp classic *Road House* (1989), produced by Joel Silver; the tear-jerking *Ghost* (1990) with Demi Moore and Whoopi Goldberg; and *Point Break* (1991), co-starring Keanu Reeves. Cast as a Californian surfing guru and part-time bank robber, Swayze looked right at home.

Father Hood was directed by Darrell James Roodt, a white South African trying his luck in Hollywood. Roodt had impressed international critics with *Jobman* (1990), a hard-edged drama about poverty, disability and ever-present racial prejudice. Roodt followed this with the anti-apartheid musical *Sarafina!* (1992), co-starring imported American Whoopi Goldberg. As Roodt's US debut, *Father Hood* is a serious let-down, misfiring on all cylinders.

Patrick Swayze stars as Jack Charles, a small-time crook, widower, absent father and all-purpose loser. When Charles' teenage daughter Kelly (Sabrina Lloyd) escapes from an abusive foster home, he is forced to rediscover his paternal instinct. Having seen Kelly's fellow inmates in handcuffs, Charles removes her young brother Eddie (Brian Bonsall) from the institution at gunpoint and goes on the run. Berry plays Kathleen Mercer, an ambitious young reporter on Charles' trail.

Uncertainly directed by Roodt, *Father Hood* lurches from heavy drama to near farce. While the flashback structure guarantees a happy ending, much of the film is extremely grim. The solid supporting cast includes Diane Ladd and Michael Ironside, who do what they can with thin characters. Scott Spencer's script attempts to deal with heavy-duty themes, including parental responsibility and the abuse of children in state foster homes. This well-intentioned, if clumsy, social pleading is countered by a frivolous approach to robbery, which looks as easy and harmless as a boy scout jaunt. Jack Charles, it seems, is not a real thief, as he only stole from drug dealers. It's poetic justice.

A charismatic if not particularly versatile actor, Swayze seems utterly lost. Playing Jack Charles in deranged rockabilly style, he turns in a manic, charmless performance. Having declared that "I hate all this family crap," Charles undergoes a conversion on the road to New Orleans. Confined to a small, poorly conceived role, Berry does a solid job, under the circumstances. A cool-but-caring investigative journalist, Kathleen Mercer is out to bust the foster care racket. Oddly, when Charles snatches his son from the juvenile hall bus, Mercer writes a sensationalist account, heavily biased in the institution's favour. Given *Father Hood*'s brief running time and choppy editing, it's possible some major sequences were cut.

As things stand, most of Kathleen Mercer's scenes involve talking to Jack Charles on the phone, which doesn't make for dynamic viewing. Convinced, for some reason, that Kathleen is Irish, Jack gets a big surprise when they finally meet at the film's conclusion. *Father Hood* proved that Halle Berry could win roles not written specifically for a black actress. Unfortunately, it was a hollow victory on this occasion.

As the Charles children, Sabrina Lloyd and Brian Bonsall emerge from *Father Hood* unscathed. Cast as a moody

teenager, Lloyd was in her early twenties at the time, only a few years younger than co-star Berry. Kelly Charles provides a voice-over narration at the start of the movie and sounds far more adult than she appears on screen. It's hinted that Kelly suffered sexual abuse while in care, though the film doesn't spell this out.

Weakly punning title aside, *Father Hood* never looked like a serious box-office contender. Marketed with the equally lame slogan 'He's America's most wanted… Dad!', the film opened in US cinemas on 27 August 1993. *Variety* summed up the general critical response: "A train wreck from start to finish." *Father Hood* proved a major flop, taking only $3.4 million at the box-office. As another nail in Patrick Swayze's movie star coffin, the film went straight-to-video in the UK.

Released less than a month after *Father Hood*, *The Program* (1993) probably looked a better bet on paper. Produced by Touchstone, Disney's 'adult' film division, this college sports exposé proved another disappointment for Halle Berry. The basic plot has served many a sporting movie: faced with impending unemployment, a football coach in charge of a loser team takes drastic action. The film starred 1970s leading man James Caan, who'd made a recent comeback in *Dick Tracy* (1990), *Misery* (1990), *For the Boys* (1991) and *Honeymoon in Vegas* (1992). The cast also included rising black actor Omar Epps and Kristy Swanson, who played *Buffy the Vampire Slayer* in the ill-fated 1992 movie. In need of a decent film role after *Father Hood*, Halle Berry signed on to play Omar Epps' love interest.

The Program was directed and co-written by David S Ward, who shot the film on location at Duke University,

Durham, in North Carolina, and at the University of South Carolina. Twenty years earlier, Ward had won an Academy Award for writing *The Sting* (1973), a slick, convoluted tale of lovable confidence tricksters. By the late 1980s, Ward specialised in broad family comedies, notably *Major League* (1989) and *King Ralph* (1991). Looking for more heavyweight material, along the lines of his earlier *Cannery Row* (1981), Ward came up with an issue-heavy movie that never works as drama. While steroid abuse remains a topical subject, the characters involved are neither interesting nor likeable.

As a piece of film-making, *The Program* is undistinguished. During the football sequences, Ward gives us point-of-view shots from inside the player's helmets. This sort of works, in a rollercoaster kind of way, though the subjective effect wears thin with repetition. As the hard-nosed Coach Winters, Caan gives a one-note portrayal, the actor clearly unimpressed with the script. Twenty-three years earlier, Caan had given one of his best performances as a football star in the TV movie *Brian's Song* (1970), the true story of Chicago Bears player Brian Piccolo and his battle with cancer.

The younger cast members fare little better, stuck with a routine plot. Star quarterback Joe Kane (Craig Sheffer) becomes involved with petite blonde Camille (Swanson), while running back Darnell Jefferson (Epps) falls for Autumn Haley (Berry). Initially resistant to Darnell's football jock charms, Autumn has an abrupt change of heart. While this makes for a happy ending, it isn't very convincing. The smart, ambitious Autumn is way out of Darnell's league and they still seem mismatched at the fade-out. Working from another weak script, Berry

struggles with her contrived, wafer-thin character. That said, her solid performance is the film's strongest asset. It comes as no surprise that director David S Ward made a rapid return to comedies with *Major League II* (1994) and *Down Periscope* (1996).

The Program opened in the United States on 24 September 1993, to mediocre reviews and lukewarm ticket sales. A few weeks into its American release, the film acquired unexpected publicity of the worst kind. One scene features the trainee football stars proving their machismo by lying down in the middle of a busy road. Several teenagers attempted a similar stunt, leading to one being killed and others badly injured. Faced with tabloid allegations of inciting copycat behaviour, Touchstone had the sequence removed from all release prints of the film. This controversy did little for *The Program*'s box-office, which stalled at $23 million.

With her movie career going nowhere in particular, Berry was offered a co-starring role in the Twentieth Century Fox production *Speed* (1994), playing plucky stand-in bus driver Angela. While *Speed* went on to be the 'sleeper' hit of the year, at the time it seemed a dubious proposition. First-time director Jan De Bont, a former cameraman on action thrillers such as *Die Hard* (1988) and *Basic Instinct* (1992), was an unknown quantity. The plot, involving a bus, a bomb and a 50mph trigger mechanism, amounted to no more than a feature-length action sequence. Leading man Keanu Reeves had a variable track record, despite hits with *Bill and Ted's Excellent Adventure* (1989), *Point Break* (1991) and *Bram Stoker's Dracula* (1992).

Dismissed by many Hollywood insiders as 'the bus movie', *Speed* didn't

RIGHT:
Halle attends the premiere for *The Flintstones* with first husband David Justice.

that I didn't feel vulnerable one bit. It was just fun…"

Opening with the legend 'Steven Spielrock Presents', *The Flintstones* begins on a lame note and never picks up. On the plus side, the production design is impressive, recreating Bedrock's rock quarry, main street and stone vehicles with uncanny accuracy. The dinosaurs, a combination of CGI effects and animatronic puppets, are cartoonish variants on the beasts of Spielberg's *Jurassic Park* (1993). The various mammoths, sabre-toothed tigers, wild boars and horny toads are equally fine. The rot sets in early, however, with tiresome references to Univershell, RocDonalds and, er, *Jurassic Park*.

One of the movie's biggest problems is the feeble script. While only three writers are credited, over 30 seasoned Hollywood hacks had a shot at 'improving' the screenplay. Aside from some okay visual gags and one-liners, including a reference to human sacrifice, the end result is poor. In terms of acting, *The Flintstones* is a non-starter. While the four leads accurately recreate the vocal inflections and mannerisms of the cartoon characters, they bring nothing extra to the roles. John Goodman looks uncannily like the original Fred Flintstone yet this is an impersonation, not a performance. Paradoxically, the two-dimensional cel animation, voiced by the late Alan Reed, is more believable.

First seen clad in a leopard-skin bikini top and sarong, Sharon Stone pours Cliff Vandercave's drink into a huge goblet. Dragging on an equally oversized cigarette, she blows a smoke ring shaped like a dollar sign. Discussing Fred Flintstone as a likely fall guy for their fraud scheme, Sharon shows that she's smarter than Cliff:

CLIFF: "He's dense. He's witless."
SHARON: "He's perfect."

Swapping her leopard-skin ensemble for black bear fur, then giraffe hide, Sharon certainly knows how to power-dress. Appointed Flintstone's secretary, she slinks into his office accompanied by a raunchy solo saxophone. As Fred's tongue lolls, Sharon gives him the sweet talk: "Feel free to use me however you see fit." In truth, this is not a very dignified part, Sharon filing her nails and swinging her arse. While she is clearly putting on an act for Flintstone, it's still tacky. Naturally, the good-natured Fred changes Sharon's attitude. Realising that Cliff plans to doublecross her, Sharon then changes sides, knocking Vandercave cold with his own flight bag.

It's notable that *The Flintstone*'s only major black character is a villain, albeit one who reforms. Perhaps with this in mind, the producers also feature a black adoption agency worker. Arrested for embezzlement and forgery, Sharon seems only semi-repentant: "I've been a very bad girl. But you have to admit, I was very, very good at it." Appropriately, Berry's performance was rewarded with a 1995 MTV Movie Award nomination for Most Desirable Female.

The Flintstones opened in the United States on 27 May 1994, earning some dismal reviews. Critics vied for the best snappy put-down, *USA Today* winning the contest with "Yabba Dabba Don't." British audiences had to wait until 22 July, by which time Universal's marketing department was working overtime to promote the movie.

The Flintstones took $130.5 million in North America alone and $358.5 million worldwide.

LEFT:
The Flintstones. Sharon Stone (Halle Berry) models the latest in prehistoric fashion.

CRITICAL DECISIONS

STILL awaiting her big Hollywood break, Halle Berry was lured back to television for a co-starring role in *Solomon and Sheba* (1995). Produced by Showtime Networks Inc., this Old Testament saga of love, loss and the Almighty seemed a strange career move. Cast as Nikhaule, also known as the Queen of Sheba, Berry at least got to play one of the Bible's more memorable female characters.

The director, Robert M Young, had laboured in television for nearly 30 years, turning out scripts for *Columbo, Kojak, Harry O, Cannon, Barnaby Jones* and *Night Gallery*. A respected documentary maker, Young's intermittent feature films included the worthy social dramas *Rich Kids* (1979) and *Dominick and Eugene* (1988). Scriptwriter Ronni Kern had worked on the films *A Change of Seasons* (1980), a mid-life crisis comedy starring Anthony Hopkins and Shirley MacLaine, and Ralph Bakshi's *American Pop* (1981), an ambitious animated history of American music. More recently employed on *Baywatch*, Kern didn't seem the obvious choice for a biblical epic.

The role of Solomon went to Jimmy Smits, taking time off from his popular TV show *NYPD Blue* (1994-98). The supporting cast featured some fine British actors, notably Kenneth Colley, Nickolas Grace, Hugh Quarshie and Nadia Sawalha. Credited as 'First Prostitute', Sawalha probably doesn't count *Solomon and Sheba* as a career highpoint.

Solomon and Sheba has little to recommend it. The production is afflicted by the same deathly reverence found in many of Hollywood's biblical epics. Jimmy Smits' Solomon looks like *NYPD Blue*'s Detective Bobby Simone under very deep cover. While Berry seems more at home, dressed in a fine selection of authentic Old Testament outfits, she can't bring the stilted dialogue to life. The dull end result is no great improvement on the stilted 1959 epic starring Yul Brynner and Gina Lollobrigida. First broadcast in the US on 26 February 1995, *Solomon and Sheba* quickly faded into obscurity, though Berry's performance earned a 1996 Image Award nomination for Outstanding Actress in a Television Movie, Mini-Series or Drama Special.

Berry returned to feature films with the Paramount production *Losing Isaiah* (1995). Discarding the Queen of Sheba's regal trappings, she played Khaila Richards, a single mother and reformed drug abuser who attempts to regain custody of her young son. *Losing Isaiah* is the great might-have-been of Berry's career, the film she hoped would make her name as both an actress and a star.

Based on a novel by Seth Margolis, *Losing Isaiah* was made by the husband-and-wife team of director Stephen Gyllenhaal and producer-writer Naomi Foner. Following an impressive feature debut with *Paris Trout* (1991), a dark Deep South tale starring Dennis Hopper, Gyllenhaal recruited Foner for *A Dangerous Woman* (1993), an offbeat small-town drama providing good roles for Debra Winger and Barbara Hershey. Gyllenhaal also worked in television, directing episodes of *Twin Peaks* (1990) and *Homicide: Life on the Streets* (1993).

Berry's co-stars in *Losing Isaiah*

RIGHT: Halle in *Solomon and Sheba*, a little-seen television movie.

33

included Jessica Lange; David Straithairn, who'd appeared in *A Dangerous Woman*; *Jungle Fever*'s Samuel L Jackson and a rising young actor named Cuba Gooding Jr. Desperate to win the part of Khaila Richards, Berry found she faced an uphill struggle. As Gyllenhaal later admitted to *Toronto Sun* reporter Bruce Kirkland: "I saw nothing in her work that suggested she could do this. I assumed she couldn't handle it. I was wrong!" In fairness, Berry had yet to play a major film role, though her performance in the television drama *Queen* suggested a talent that went beyond mere looks. Gyllenhaal auditioned Berry purely out of professional courtesy, both to the actress and her agents. Berry realised that the director was unconvinced, telling Kirkland:

> I knew there was a lot of scepticism. I can be honest with myself and realise why. My career is very new. I haven't proven myself in many ways. I haven't had the opportunity.

Berry also appreciated that both Gyllenhaal and Paramount were taking a risk with *Losing Isaiah*'s contentious subject matter. Neither director nor studio would compromise the film by miscasting a crucial lead role: "...I can understand how he felt. I understand that this is a big movie for Paramount and a big deal for him as a director."

Having invited Berry to audition out of politeness, Gyllenhaal was surprised at her passion and dramatic power. Called back for a second audition, Berry felt she'd blown her chances: "...I came in too emotional. I was just a wreck because I wanted it so badly." In fact, Berry had become a serious contender for the role, which appealed to her on several levels:

I wanted this chance to prove that I could do this. As a black woman, roles like this just aren't around... I think the issue is something that I felt really passionate about. It is important to me that I'm part of something that may help incite change. We provide no answers. It's no easy subject.

ABOVE:
Losing Isaiah. Khaila Richards (Halle Berry) attempts to bond with estranged son Isaiah (Marc John Jeffries).

Having won the part of Khaila Richards, Berry undertook extensive research into the lives of crack cocaine addicts, an area she'd already covered with her small role in *Jungle Fever*. Praising Berry as an intelligent, gifted performer, Gyllenhaal tipped her as a future star.

Budgeted at a modest $17 million, *Losing Isaiah* was filmed on location in Chicago, Illinois. Still a dedicated method actor, Berry looked to her own troubled background to bring Khaila Richards alive:

BELOW:
Losing Isaiah. Khaila attends the court hearing with lawyer Kadar Lewis (Samuel L Jackson).

...for a lot of the scenes, I had to really draw on some of the pain in my life, and revisit that time, live there for a while and bring all of that stuff up and try to channel it into Khaila in the best way that I could.

Working with a difficult, emotionally draining character, Berry found the shoot painful in other ways. During production, a make-up woman managed to scratch Berry's corneas while applying eye drops. Left in extreme discomfort, Berry had to stop work, which played havoc with the film's tight schedule. Seven years later, Berry would suffer another on-set eye injury while filming *Die Another Day* (2002).

Shortly before *Losing Isaiah* went on release, Berry expressed her strong feelings for the film:

It's like my baby. I don't want bad things said about it. I don't want anyone to hurt it. I want it to be good. It's something I'm proud of.

Unfortunately, the finished film doesn't justify Berry's commitment. Well-intentioned to the nth degree, *Losing Isaiah* plays as a deluxe TV movie. Khaila Richards abandons her baby son, Isaiah, at the height of her drug addiction and believes him to be dead. In fact, the authorities have placed Isaiah with a white middle-class couple, who offer financial and emotional stability. Discovering that her son is still alive, Khaila hires black lawyer Kadar Lewis (Samuel L Jackson) to get him back. Attempting to explore sensitive racial and cultural issues, the film never comes to life as drama. Screenwriter Naomi Foner offers crude stereotypes rather than rounded characters. The thin, contrived story is neither convincing nor involving.

Losing Isaiah is partially salvaged by its cast, though some of the acting is embarrassingly misjudged. Jessica Lange gives a forceful performance as Margaret Lewin, a social worker who 'rescued' Isaiah from a life in institutions. Playing her second crack cocaine addict, Berry lends both passion and conviction to an underwritten character. An illiterate

street junkie, Khaila is first seen attempting to breast-feed Isaiah. Unable to control her drug craving, she leaves her baby in a trash can and goes on the hunt for a dealer. Stripped of all glamour, Berry has wild hair and a bad attitude.

Arrested for shoplifting, Khaila is placed in a rehabilitation programme. These scenes, which should be extremely powerful, are clichéd and overwrought, verging on the absurd. That said, Berry gets plenty of chances to show that she can cry believably on camera. Cleaned up and relocated to a housing project, Khaila learns to read and becomes involved with a neighbour, Eddie Hughes (Cuba Gooding Jr).

While Berry wins some sympathy for her character, she gets little help from the script. Khaila is not particularly likeable, despite her successful battle with drug addiction. Assuming that Isaiah is hers by right, she tends to forget that he's not a possession. As one character delicately puts it: "Just because you fucked some junkie on a street corner doesn't make you his mother." For the record, child actor Marc John Jefferies is very engaging as Isaiah

The film turns into a prolonged courtroom drama, placing interracial adoption in the dock. Berry plays these scenes well, with solid support from Samuel L Jackson, a good friend off screen. In truth, Khaila's eventual

ABOVE:
Losing Isaiah. Khaila resists the attentions of smooth-talking Eddie Hughes (Cuba Gooding Jnr).

RIGHT:
Executive Decision. Plucky flight attendant Jean (Halle Berry) keeps a watchful eye on terrorist Nagi Hassan (David Suchet).

victory will strike some viewers as the wrong verdict. A virtual stranger to Isaiah, Khaila has no immediate rapport with him, suggesting that mother and son face an uncertain future.

Marketed with the tagline 'Who decides what makes a mother?', *Losing Isaiah* opened in the United States on 17March 1995. Paramount drummed up all the publicity they could around the film's controversial theme, yet *Losing Isaiah* never became a must-see event movie. Making little impression on either critics or audiences, the film grossed only $7.6 million. The overseas theatrical receipts amounted to a meagre $900,000. *Losing Isaiah* didn't reach Britain until June 1996, as a straight-to-video release. Berry, however, received another Image Award nomination, this time for Outstanding Lead Actress in a Motion Picture.

In urgent need of another box-office hit, Berry reunited with Warner and producer Joel Silver for *Executive Decision* (1996). This $55 million action thriller stars Kurt Russell, with a 'guest' appearance from scowling hard man Steven Seagal, and pits fearless American commandos, academics, engineers and flight attendants against ruthless Islamic terrorists. It's no contest.

The involved script for *Executive Decision* features the lethal 'DZ-5' nerve toxin, an airplane hijack and an imprisoned terrorist leader. Russell is Government Intelligence man David Grant, a PhD academic with a fine taste in evening wear. Seagal is no-nonsense army man Lieutenant Colonel Austin Travis, who leads the initial counterstrike. Character actor Oliver Platt plays Dennis Cahill, inventor of a special 'sleeve' that can connect two aircraft in flight. British actor David Suchet accepted the role of chief Arab terrorist Nagi Hassan, a hardline follower of Islam who keeps the Koran by his side. Cast as plucky

flight attendant Jean, Berry picked up her first $1 million paycheck for the film, along with her own make-up artist, hair stylist and personal assistant.

First-time director Stuart Baird was one of the industry's most respected editors. Born in Britain, Baird began his movie career during the 1970s, working on *Tommy* (1975), *The Omen* (1976) and *Superman* (1978). Relocating to Hollywood, Baird found regular employment with producer Joel Silver, editing *Lethal Weapon, Lethal Weapon 2* (1989), *Die Hard 2* and *The Last Boy Scout*. Having taken a chance on Stuart Baird, Silver hired an experienced director of photography, Baird's fellow Briton Alex Thomson. Like Baird, Thomson began his career in England, working on the swinging sixties comedy *Here We Go Round the Mulberry Bush* (1967) and the plodding 'youth epic' *Alfred the Great* (1969). Thomson did some of his best work on the Arthurian epic *Excalibur* (1981), for which he received an Academy Award nomination. His Hollywood credits included *Legend* (1985), *High Spirits* (1988), *Alien3* (1992), *Cliffhanger* (1993) and *Demolition Man* (1993).

Aside from an overdose of scene-setting, and one dodgy disguise, *Executive Decision* is first-class entertainment, tense and well-paced. Handed the driver's seat, Baird orchestrates the hi-tech mayhem with brisk efficiency. Loaded up with DZ-5 and a very large bomb, the hijacked 747 will become a vast missile, aimed at the heart of Washington DC. If Hassan has his wicked way, half of America's Eastern Seaboard will soon be history. As Hassan puts it: "Our destiny is to deliver the vengeance of Allah into the belly of the Infidel."

The script attempts a few shades of grey: not all Hassan's fellow hijackers are ruthless killers, and an American politician on board the plane tries to exploit the crisis for his own advancement. Given the events of 11 September 2001, this silly, if gripping, action fantasy now looks oddly prescient. The movie's one big 'twist' is killing off Seagal's character early on, Austin Travis nobly sacrificing himself for the sake of the mission. At least he got to kill a few bad guys first.

Despite her second billing, Berry doesn't have much to do in *Executive Decision*. Looking smart in her navy blue uniform, Jean is certainly brave, hiding the crucial passenger list from Hassan. Concerned for the people on board, especially the children, Jean refuses to be cowed by the terrorist. A fellow flight attendant, blonde and neurotic, just looks helpless. Jean finds Hassan's hand-drawn plan for the Washington attack and helps David Grant organise a counter-attack. While the commandos are dubious, Grant knows that Jean is up to the job.

Looking for an incognito terrorist holding the remote bomb trigger, she fingers the wrong guy, a non-fanatical diamond smuggler. Luckily, David doesn't hold it against her. Suffering for her patriotism, Jean gets whacked in the face by Hassan, who also points a gun at her head. He's no gentleman. Having helped Grant land the plane, Jean accepts his offer of a coffee. The film ends with a throwaway joke about Berry's marriage to baseball player David Justice. It probably doesn't seem so funny now.

Released in the United States on 15 March 1996, *Executive Decision* took $68 million at the box-office, eventually matched by another $65.4 million from overseas. While $133.4 million sounds an impressive total, the film turned only a small profit once the costs of marketing and distribution had been covered. *Executive Decision* opened in British cinemas on 10 May, the British Board of Film Classification having requested eight seconds of cuts before granting the film a '15' certificate. Seagal's dextrous knife-play was

ABOVE:
Race the Sun.
Miss Sandra Beecher
(Halle Berry),
inspirational
teacher.

the main casualty, the BBFC being concerned about impressionable teenagers reaching for the kitchen drawer. While *Executive Decision* picked up few accolades, Berry's spirited performance won her the 1997 Blockbuster Entertainment Award for Favourite Actress – Adventure/Drama. How's this for a movie pitch? A group of deprived, ethnically diverse high school kids from Hawaii compete in an international solar-powered car race. It's an inspirational, feel-good movie where the underdog wins out against the odds. Columbia TriStar obviously liked the idea, giving *Race the Sun* (1996) the green light.

The film was directed by Charles T. Kanganis, whose previous work included the uninspiring *3 Ninjas Kick Back* (1994). Screenwriter Barry Morrow

had more impressive credits, notably the book *Bill*, the true-life story of a retarded man forced to cope with the outside world after 40 years in an institution. *Bill* became an acclaimed 1981 TV movie starring Mickey Rooney. A specialist in disability issues, Morrow subsequently co-scripted *Rain Man* (1988), which starred Dustin Hoffman as an autistic man. Both Hoffman and the screenplay won Academy Awards, though the latter was stronger on sentiment than dramatic force. Morrow based his script for *Race the Sun* on the 1990 World Solar Challenge, held in Australia.

Berry agreed to play Miss Sandra Beecher, the high school teacher who encourages her poor-yet-promising pupils to give it their best shot. The kids were led by Casey Affleck, brother of the better-known Ben, and Eliza Dushku. Affleck had recently played a more sinister teenager in Gus Van Sant's *To Die For* (1995), falling under the spell of Nicole Kidman's murderously ambitious weather girl. Dushku's biggest movie to date was the spy thriller *True Lies* (1994), which cast her as Arnold Schwarzenegger's stroppy adolescent daughter. Eliza Dushku later achieved small screen celebrity in *Buffy the Vampire Slayer*, playing renegade slayer Faith. The cast also included Sara Tanaka, who subsequently appeared in *Rushmore* (1998), a much sharper take on those difficult teenage years.

Looking for some more familiar adult faces, the producers settled on James Belushi, younger brother of the deceased comedy star John Belushi. Twelfth-billed on *Race the Sun*, Belushi comes and goes to no great effect. The Australian acting contingent was headed by veteran thespian Bill Hunter, recently seen in the home-grown hits

Strictly Ballroom (1992) and
Muriel's Wedding (1994).

Race the Sun is predictable,
forgettable whimsy, where the white
villain dresses in black and sports
decidedly Aryan blond hair. The
Australian locations, which include
Adelaide and Sydney, are well used.
Inevitably, the kids learn to believe in
themselves and fulfil their potential. As
the tagline put it: 'A dream can make all

the difference under the sun.' While the
moral lesson is fine, worthy intentions
do not necessarily make for a good
movie. As the inspirational Sandra
Beecher, Berry looks good in a grass
skirt. Opening in the United States
on 22 March 1996, *Race the Sun* died at
the box-office, grossing a pitiful $1.7
million. Needless to say, the film went
straight-to-video in Britain.

Five years after *Jungle Fever*, Berry

ABOVE: *Race the
Sun*. Sandra Beecher
with Frank Machi
(James Belushi).

played another small role in a Spike Lee film, *Girl 6* (1996). Made in partnership with Twentieth Century Fox, *Girl 6* stars Theresa Randle, who'd appeared in *CB4*, as unemployed New York actress Judy, who finds a new career in telephone sex. A curious blend of satire and fantasy, the film is also heavy on in-jokes. In one scene, Judy performs a monologue from *She's Gotta Have It*, Lee's debut feature film. Elsewhere, Lee plays with racial, gender and cultural stereotypes, to no great purpose.Grateful to Lee for her break in *Jungle Fever*, Berry agreed to play a cameo role. The starry supporting cast also includes Naomi Campbell, Quentin Tarantino and Madonna.

Theresa Randle's numerous impersonations in the film include tragic black actress Dorothy Dandridge, one of Berry's idols, and blaxploitation icon Pam Grier. Three years later, Berry gave a more heavyweight portrayal of the former in *Introducing Dorothy Dandridge*. Oddly enough, Berry would also be asked to star in a remake of *Foxy Brown* (1974), one of Grier's definitive vehicles.

Opening in the United States on 22 March 1996, the same day as *Race the Sun*, *Girl 6* did a little better at the box-office, taking $4.9 million. That said, *Jungle Fever* had grossed over six times that figure five years earlier. *Girl 6* opened in the UK on 7 June.

Berry secured another leading role in *The Rich Man's Wife* (1996). Intended as a thriller, this Hollywood/Buena Vista production fails on all counts. Whatever Berry's hopes for the film, she can't have felt the same sense of commitment that inspired her on *Losing Isaiah*. *Rich Man's Wife* was written and directed by

Amy Holden Jones, whose eclectic credits ranged from the gory slasher movie *Slumber Party Massacre* (1982) to the sickly-sweet *Beethoven* series. Berry's co-stars included British actor Clive Owen, who'd attracted attention in the incest drama *Close My Eyes* (1990), and Peter Greene, the chief villain in *The Mask* (1994).

Rich Man's Wife is set in the affluent district of Malibu, California. Berry plays Josie Potenza, a young woman trapped in an unhappy marriage. Seeking refuge in an extramarital affair with neighbour Jake Golden (Owen), Josie also hangs around bars. On one such excursion, she encounters resident psycho nutter Cole Wilson (Greene) and drunkenly confides her marital woes. Just a few scenes later, Tony Potenza (Christopher McDonald) is murdered. Having wished her wealthy husband dead in the presence of witnesses, Josie becomes the chief suspect and must fight to clear her name. Aside from her troubles with the law, Josie is being stalked, Cole subjecting her to a campaign of blackmail, housebreaking and assault. There's a further twist: could Josie's lover Jake also be mixed up in Tony's murder?

Employing a familiar flashback structure, Amy Holden Jones' film never strays from the predictable. Interviewed by the police, Josie tells her story, sometimes referring to events and conversations she could not have witnessed first-hand. Unable to whip up much tension or suspense, Holden Jones delivers a ludicrous woman-in-peril melodrama, with a few reasonable jolts. The performances are similarly disappointing. Clive Owen, a gifted actor, is badly miscast, turning Jake into a major irritation. In fairness, Owen soon redeemed himself with the British production *Croupier* (1997), a 'sleeper' hit in the United States.

As the nominal star of *Rich Man's Wife*, Berry is by no means at her best. Restricting her facial expressions to fear and despair, Berry often looks eager to be elsewhere. It's likely the role of Josie was conceived with a white actress in mind, which may have attracted Berry to the part. As it is, she delivers lines like "I really did love my husband" with minimum conviction. Viewers unfamiliar with Berry's earlier work no doubt left the cinema with little impression of her talent. The sharpest performance comes from Clea Lewis, stuck in the thankless part of Nora Golden, Jake's deceived wife. Best known for her co-starring role in the sitcom *Ellen*, Lewis adds a welcome touch of comedy relief to the grim proceedings.

Advertised with the tagline 'The price of wealth just went up', *The Rich Man's Wife* hit US cinemas on 13 September 1996. While the film remained on release until 5 January 1997, it grossed only $8.538 million. Faced with poor box-office returns in the United States, Buena Vista's overseas offices added *Rich Man's Wife* to their 'video premiere' pile. In Britain, the film hit the video rental stores in May 1997, making little impression.

Berry could shrug off the commercial failure of *The Rich Man's Wife*, yet her real-life marriage to David Justice was in a bad state. In March 1996, the couple separated after three years together. The following month, Berry filed for divorce, accusing Justice of serial infidelity. When Justice was questioned by the police on suspicion of kerb-crawling, Berry decided she'd had enough. Interviewed by the press,

Justice claimed that Berry, now his ex-wife, had a bad temper and a suspicious mind. In October 1996, Berry sought a restraining order against Justice, citing fears for her personal safety.

Despite Berry's obvious anger at Justice's betrayal, their break-up left her in a state of despair. On one particularly bad night, she supposedly walked into her garage, closed the door, got inside her car and started the engine. As the lethal carbon monoxide fumes began to fill the garage, Berry thought of her mother Judith, who'd striven so hard to look after her and older sister Heidi. Realising that taking her own life was a selfish, thoughtless act, qualities she associated with her father, Berry switched off the engine. While Berry is reluctant to discuss this alleged incident, she admits to entertaining thoughts of suicide after the divorce. Five years later, while promoting *Monster's Ball* in Britain, Berry told journalist Robin Taylor:

> I was going to sit in the car and asphyxiate myself but I thought, "What is my mother going to think if she finds me dead in this car?"

Having reached a crossroads in her personal life, Berry found her movie career stuck in low gear. When New Line offered Berry a starring role in the comedy *B*A*P*S* (1997), she had little option but to accept. Seldom has a gifted performer been so thoroughly wasted. A Cinderella tale of two Georgia home girls who get lucky in LA, *B*A*P*S* should have stayed in the studio's reject pile.

The film's black director, Robert Townsend, had similar career problems to Halle Berry. A talented stand-up comic, Townsend broke into movies as

ABOVE:
Rich Man's Wife.
Josie Potenza (Halle
Berry) has good
reason to look over
her shoulder.

a supporting actor, appearing in *A Soldier's Story* (1984) and *Streets of Fire* (1984), a Joel Silver production that also featured *Flintstones* star Rick Moranis. Townsend enjoyed his biggest film success as the writer-director-producer-

star of *Hollywood Shuffle* (1987). A labour of love, this minor classic satirises the way black actors are still stereotyped in movies as muggers, pimps, studs, whores, rapists and general low-life. Shot over several years on a minuscule budget, *Hollywood Shuffle* drew on a wealth of black talent, including brother performers Keenan Ivory Wayans and Damon Wayans. The film's success secured Townsend the directing gig on *Eddie Murphy Raw* (1987), Murphy's attempt to emulate the success of Richard Pryor's stand-up movies.

Unfortunately, Townsend's subsequent films as a writer-director proved disappointing, suggesting that the energy, inspiration and passion of his debut was a one-off. While *The Five Heartbeats* (1991), a clichéd showbiz saga about a 1960s singing group, has its moments, *Meteor Man* (1992) is a weak superhero spoof. Five years later, Townsend signed on for *B*A*P*S* as a director for hire, making no contribution to the script.

The screenplay for *B*A*P*S* was written by Troy Beyer, a black actress who'd appeared in Townsend's *Five Heartbeats*. Four years older than Berry, Beyer took a similar route into movies through television, appearing in *Sesame Street* and *Dynasty*. Beyer got an early small screen break in *Knots Landing*, six years before Berry's one-season stint on the show. Beyer's other film credits included *Disorderlies* (1987), a vehicle for overweight black rappers The Fat Boys, and *Weekend at Bernie's II* (1993), probably the least necessary sequel of all time.

B*A*P*S was Beyer's first filmed screenplay and it's a mystery what anyone saw in it. In fact, the film's plot bears a suspicious resemblance to *Disorderlies*. Both feature an elderly white millionaire, a scheming nephew and a team of heroic soul brothers/sisters who shake up the joint and put things right. Still, after ten years on the shelf, such a strong concept just had to be recycled. For

the record, the title stands for Black American Princesses.

Berry co-starred in *B*A*P*S* opposite newcomer Natalie Desselle, who had only one previous film credit, a bit part in *Set It Off* (1996), a superior ghetto action drama starring Jada Pinkett Smith. For *B*A*P*S*, Desselle received an 'Introducing' credit, which did her no favours. The supporting cast included respected actors Martin Landau and Ian Richardson.

Right from the start, *B*A*P*S* looks a bust. Denise, or 'Nisi' (Berry), is a waitress at Johnson's Soul Food Heaven diner. Adorned with absurdly long fingernails and a blonde wig, she also sports a gold tooth and huge ear-rings. Her best friend is the dumpy yet feisty Mickey (Desselle), who requires big portions of everything. A failed hairdresser, Nisi has big Hollywood dreams. Unfortunately, her boyfriend, high school sweetheart Ali (Pierre Edwards), is a loser with a bad perm. Determined to win the Video Dance Girl of the World competition and star in a pop video with Heavy D, Nisi and Mickey head for Los Angeles.

Once in the City of Angels, Nisi models ever more absurd hair and clothes, including a shiny orange two-piece with high heels. Befriended by the dubious Isaac (Jonathan Fried), the ladies hang at a Beverly Hills mansion, where Nisi tries out her knowledge of etiquette. Informed by Isaac that his wealthy uncle, Mr Blakemore (Landau), is dying, Nisi agrees to a little deception. She will pose as the granddaughter of Blakemore's lost love, granting his last wish. Or something like that. Nisi and Mickey turn Mr Blakemore on to soul food and Ice Cube, giving him a new lease of life. They also loosen up Manley (Richardson), a haughty butler with a passion for daytime soap operas. Mickey becomes interested in Antonio (Luigi Amodeo), a suave Euro-boy with a touch of the Latin lover. That said, she's saving herself for the wedding night.

Boasting a medium funky soundtrack, B*A*P*S has few other redeeming features. Townsend's technically competent direction lacks any sense of pace or comic timing. In the ten years since *Hollywood Shuffle*, something had gone badly wrong. The ramshackle narrative suggests heavy post-production cutting, though the movie is still painfully drawn out. The depiction of African-Americans is less than flattering, even allowing for a sense of irony. Hanging at The Gold Tooth nightclub, black men are depicted as penniless lechers. Troy Beyer's script is truly dreadful at times, treating the main characters as near-simpletons. Nisi and Mickey laugh at a statue's small penis, mock a Picasso portrait and prove clueless with a bidet. The water jet shoots suggestively between Nisi's legs as she slips and slides around the bathroom.

Beyer, who also appears in the film as Blakemore's lawyer, attempts to give the proceedings a little depth, touching on interracial love, social prejudice and moral dilemmas. Having become fond of Mr Blakemore, Nisi feels guilty about the scam: "We waiting around for some man to die. It don't feel right." But too much of the film is filled with water polo, shopping sprees, posh restaurants and mass dancing.

The cast struggle through with dogged professionalism. As Mr Blakemore, Martin Landau is both sad and spooky, though he hits the dance floor with enthusiasm. As Nisi, Berry gives a game but misjudged performance, described by *Time*

Out reviewer Nick Bradshaw as "desperately goofy". While Nisi and Mickey are supposed to be decent people, the film treats them as caricatures. At least they're no pushovers, beating up a masked intruder who turns out to be Antonio. Outraged to learn that Isaac wants Mr Blakemore declared mentally incompetent, they turn down his bribe of $50,000 apiece.

B*A*P*S turns very sentimental during its final section, with no real attempt at laughs. Declaring that "There is no fortune worth the loss of a true love," Blakemore dies happy. Left fortunes in the old man's will, Nisi and Mickey have a group hug with butler Manley, while Ali shapes up and cuts his hair. Ominously, the closing title reads 'The End And The Beginning'.

B*A*P*S opened in the United States on 28 March 1997, grossing a measly $7.24 million. Surprisingly, New Line opted to give the film a theatrical release in Britain, suggesting they were short of product at the time. B*A*P*S hit the UK on 1 August, leaving most reviewers gobsmacked. As *Guardian* critic Derek Malcolm put it: "Words cannot convey the multi-hued frightfulness of this film." The movie made many critics' top ten 'Worst' lists for 1997. Berry, however, received a Best Actress nomination at the 1998 Acapulco Black Film Festival. This probably says more about the dearth of starring roles for black actors than the jury's taste.

Troy Beyer returned to movies the following year as the writer, director and co-star of *Let's Talk About Sex* (1998). A frank look at black female sexuality, the film had to be toned down to secure an 'R' rating. It's gotta be a better bet than B*A*P*S.

ABOVE: Nisi (Halle
Berry) and Mickey
(Natalie Desselle)
strut their stuff
in *BAPS*.

LEFT: Halle puts
a brave face on
in *BAPS*.

KEEPING THE FAITH

WITH her movie career in questionable shape, Halle Berry opted to revive her fortunes on the small screen. Five years earlier, she'd enjoyed one of her strongest roles in *Queen* (1993). Hoping to repeat this success, Berry agreed to star in *The Wedding* (1998). Like *Queen*, this was a lavish three-hour mini-series based on a popular novel, another multi-generational saga of African-American life.

The project was initiated by black media star Oprah Winfrey, occasional actress, daytime talk show phenomenon and cultural icon. Serving as executive producer, Winfrey made *The Wedding* through her own production company, Harpo Films Inc. The series is also known as *Oprah Winfrey Presents: The Wedding*, a clear indication of its main selling point. Citing Winfrey as one of her inspirations, Berry welcomed the opportunity to work with her.

The Wedding is based on a novel by the late Dorothy West, who drew acclaim for her first book, *The Living Is Easy* (1948). West took nearly 30 years to complete *The Wedding*, which didn't get published until 1995, when she was 88. The book follows the lives of affluent, light-skinned black Americans living in Martha's Vineyard. Spanning several decades, *The Wedding* tackles issues of class, race and gender in an assured, if sometimes overblown, prose style.

Berry's co-stars included Eric Thal, Carl Lumbly and British actress Marianne Jean-Baptiste. Most of *The Wedding* was filmed in South Carolina, with location work in Southport and ilmington. The director, Charles

RIGHT:
The Wedding. Shelby Coles (Halle Berry) in her bridal outfit.

Burnett, was one of America's most respected black filmmakers. He first came to notice with *The Killer of Sheep* (1977), a low-budget, documentary-style account of black working-class life. Burnett's best known film is *To Sleep With Anger* (1990), which stars Danny Glover as a charismatic yet malevolent stranger who threatens to tear a family apart. Unfortunately, Burnett didn't get to make another feature film until *The Glass Shield* (1995), the more conventional story of a black LA cop dealing with departmental racism and corruption.

Berry plays Shelby Coles, the troubled mixed-race daughter of a wealthy family. Torn between a white jazz musician and a more conservative, if honourable, black suitor, Shelby just doesn't know what she wants. While *Queen*'s racial, social and cultural struggles made for compulsive viewing, Shelby Coles is a far less interesting figure. Screenwriter Lisa Jones, a relatively inexperienced talent, struggles to dramatise the book's sprawling narrative. The stock characters are deployed with little imagination, stirring up minimal viewer interest. Constrained by television censorship and the mini-series format, Burnett seems uncomfortable with the material, giving little hint of his true ability.

First broadcast in the United States on 22 February 1998, *The Wedding* failed to match *Queen*'s success. Dorothy West died later the same year. Berry's performance earned her a 1999 Image Award nomination.

After three successive movie failures, both critical and commercial, Halle Berry's long, slow rise to stardom seemed to have stalled. While films like *The Flintstones* and *Executive Decision* kept Berry in the public eye, she was just one small part of a high-concept blockbuster package. What she needed was a solid dramatic vehicle that showcased the talent hinted at in *Jungle Fever*. This finally came along in the shape of *Bulworth* (1998), arguably Berry's best film.

A political satire set on the eve of the 1996 presidential elections, *Bulworth* was a pet project for producer-writer-director-star Warren Beatty. Hangin' in the LA 'hood, Beatty's jaded, suicidal Democrat senator rediscovers his passion for both politics and life. For all its flaws, *Bulworth* is a potent attack on corporate corruption, political apathy and bad movies.

A movie star for 35 years, Warren Beatty showed ambition early on, producing and starring in the 'sleeper' hit *Bonnie and Clyde* (1967). Inclined towards Big Themes, Beatty had already tackled American politics in *Shampoo* (1975), which blended its barbed satire with a more audience-friendly sex-comedy. As a director, Beatty's most ambitious project was *Reds* (1981), a biopic of American journalist and Communist sympathiser John Reed. Rewarded with a handful of Academy Awards, the movie nevertheless failed to recover its huge production costs. Inactive in movies for most of the 1980s, Beatty enjoyed a minor hit with the long-delayed *Dick Tracy* (1990), based on the popular comic-strip character.

Beatty sold his *Bulworth* idea to Twentieth Century Fox, who agreed to a relatively modest $30 million budget. The project began life as *Tribulations* before switching to the main character's name. Beatty assembled a high-calibre supporting cast, including Don Cheadle, Oliver Platt (who'd appeared in *Executive Decision*), Paul Sorvino, Jack Warden and Laurie Metcalf. Cast as the mysterious Nina, Berry got on well with Beatty during the *Bulworth* shoot and they remain good friends. Berry even assisted Beatty with his producing chores on the film, which stood her in good stead for *Introducing Dorothy Dandridge*.

Faced with another election campaign filled with media hype, empty promises and blatant hypocrisy, long-serving senator Jay Billington Bulworth (Beatty) decides he's had enough. Tired of being a corporate puppet, Bulworth arranges to have himself assassinated, first setting up a large insurance payout for his daughter. Now with nothing to lose, Bulworth refuses to tow the party line, speaking the often brutal truth for the first time in his political career. Having campaigned on an anti-positive discrimination ticket, Bulworth becomes a spokesman for ethnic minorities. Attending a church rally in LA's South Central district, Bulworth tells the black community what they have long suspected: the political establishment doesn't give a damn about them unless there are votes to be won. Dismissing initial protests, he puts his party's case very clearly: "So what are you going to do, vote Republican?"

Bulworth's now appreciative audience includes Nina, who takes the suddenly hip senator clubbing. Relaxing with a joint, Bulworth still lacks natural rhythm. Flushed with his soul-cleansing outburst, new-found popularity and a strong desire to get into Nina's pants, Bulworth now wants to live. Unfortunately, there's still the small matter of the death contract.

Repeating his campaign mantra *ad nauseam* ("We stand at the doorstep of a new millennium"), Bulworth is clearly a man on the edge, gulping down the airline whisky miniatures. Beatty dares to look old and sad, even crying during the opening sequence. Trying his hand as a club mix-master, Bulworth walks into posts, falls into ponds and takes on a racist cop. In one scene, Bulworth dresses up as a home boy, which the media interprets as a brilliant change of image. There's even a Bulworth rap, which goes on too long, though the message is strong.

Nina is first seen in the church congregation, sucking on a lollipop. Sporting mini-dreadlocks and a black halterneck waistcoat, she looks pretty cool. Playing hard to get, Nina dismisses Bulworth's initial advances with "Yo, later." Donning a parking valet jacket, she crunches an expensive car, then abruptly quits the job. Probably for the best. Significantly, Nina makes the first romantic move, coming on to Bulworth after he meets her extended family. The daughter of a Black Panther, Nina knows her socio-political history, discussing fallen leaders such as Huey Newton.

Fifty minutes into *Bulworth*, Nina is revealed as the assassin's accomplice. This could have been a cheap plot twist but it works surprisingly well. A career womaniser, Bulworth assumed that Nina had succumbed to his charisma and power. In fact, she just wanted to get him on his own. Like Cory in *The Last Boy Scout*, Nina has a noble motive for her mercenary behaviour. Her useless brother owes serious money to the local gangster, L.D. (Don Cheadle), and the $10,000 fee will settle the debt.

Having discovered the decent person beneath the cracking PR veneer, Nina really does fall for Bulworth. Choosing love over death, she even hands him her gun, the ultimate gesture of trust: "I changed my mind." When the senator becomes uncertain of their relationship, Nina is reassuring: "…You know you my nigger." Unfortunately, Jay Billington Bulworth is now too dangerous for the vested political and business interests. This outspoken, hugely popular loose cannon has to be silenced.

Realising that *Bulworth* needed careful handling, Twentieth Century Fox gave the film a showcase launch. *Bulworth* opened in the United States on 15 May 1998, playing on just two screens. Ten days later, on 25 May, the film went into wide release. Whether or not this tactic worked is open to question. Despite some highly favourable reviews, *Bulworth* grossed only $26.5 million in US cinemas, $3.5 million less than its production cost.

Bulworth opened in Britain on 22 January 1999, with Beatty hitting the chat shows to plug his movie. Handed a restrictive '18' certificate, *Bulworth* never really caught on with UK audiences. It did, however, score a success with most critics. *Time Out* reviewer Gilbert Adair praised the film as "…a sharp, brave movie … Intriguing, intelligent and ambitious". *Sight and Sound* critic Richard Kelly acclaimed *Bulworth* as "One of the best films to emerge from a Hollywood studio in the 90s." Even *The Sun* gave it the thumbs-up: "The most dangerous political satire in years." The screenplay, credited to Beatty and Jeremy Pikser, was later nominated for an Academy Award. Berry received a 1999 Image Award nomination for Outstanding Lead Actress in a Motion Picture.

Bulworth marked Berry's triumphant return to quality films after a run of poor choices. The same year, *People Magazine* voted Berry one of their 50 Most Beautiful People. She made the list again four years later, by which

time there were a few more trophies on the shelf. 1998 also saw Berry's love-life pick up when she met musician Eric Benet, from Milwaukee, Wisconsin. Attending one of Benet's concerts, Berry ran into a friend, who took her backstage to meet Benet. Interviewed by David A Keeps, Berry recalled this first encounter: "I thought he was better looking up close, and really nice." A widower, Eric Benet had lost his wife in a car crash and now raised their young daughter, India, alone. Whatever Berry's reservations about becoming an unofficial stepmother, her relationship with Benet flourished.

Involved with a musician in real life, Halle Berry got up close and personal with a troubled pop legend for her next movie. In *Why Do Fools Fall in Love* (1998), three very different women fight over the estate of Frankie Lymon, a long dead doo-wop singer. Each claims to be Lymon's legal widow, entitled to a $4 million inheritance.

Based on a real 1980s court case, the film is not a conventional biopic of Lymon, a one-hit wonder whose brief life followed the grim rise-and-fall pattern. Barely 13 when he hit the big time with The Teenagers, Lymon found adult success elusive, his career, and life, soon falling apart. He died in 1968, at age 26, from a drug overdose. Produced by Rhino Films, with distribution through Warner Bros, *Why Do Fools* has an intriguing premise, yet never really clicks. The title is taken from Lymon's best-known song, a 1955 chart hit. Ironically, most people are more familiar with the Diana Ross cover version.

Why Do Fools Fall In Love began shooting in October 1997. The location work included a trip to Florida, with scenes filmed in Jacksonville and

RIGHT:
Why Do Fools in Love? Halle as pop star widow Zola Taylor.

50

Starke. The director, Gregory Nava, had made his name with the downbeat drama *El Norte* (1983), which he also co-wrote. A decade on, he directed the less successful *My Family* (1994), a multi-generational saga starring Jimmy Smits and a young Jennifer Lopez.

Beginning in the mid-1980s, the film flashes back to the 50s and 60s as Lymon (Larenz Tate) progresses from teen singing sensation to drug-addled burn-out. The three 'wives' are a singer, schoolteacher and petty thief. Berry plays Zola Taylor, who sang with The Platters. Taylor first meets Lymon when their respective groups perform on one of DJ Alan Freed's rock specials. While their on-off relationship proves rocky, Zola Taylor believes she knew – and loved – Lymon best.

Berry identified with Zola's predicament, telling Tyler McLeod:

What woman hasn't been a fool in love? I understood the dynamic of loving a man and letting him go, taking him and loving him anyway. I've lived all that.

Unfortunately, Berry's committed performance is not matched by the rest of the film. The script, by jobbing actress Tina Andrews, plays fast and loose with the facts, offering little insight into Lymon himself. Anxious to keep things relatively upbeat, the movie glosses over the seedier aspects of Lymon's life, notably his fatal heroin addiction. While Larenz Tate offers a fair impersonation of Lymon, the scenes featuring the singer in action ring false. Berry aside, *Why Do Fools* is enlivened by a cameo from genuine singing legend Little Richard. Predictably, Lymon's three 'widows' are bonded by the experience, something which did not happen in real life.

Why Do Fools Fall in Love received its world premiere at the Urbanworld Film Festival on 8 August 1998. The film went on general release in the United States on 28 September, making the movie top ten. Other films in the charts included *How Stella Got Her Groove Back* and *Dance with Me*, starring the African-American actresses Angela Bassett and Vanessa L. Williams. Despite its top ten placing, *Why Do Fools Fall in Love* took only $12.4 million at the US box-office. Though less than half of *Bulworth*'s domestic gross, it still marked a step up from Berry's other recent films. In Britain, *Why Do Fools* premiered as another straight-to-video release.

Following her cameo appearances in *CB4* (1993) and *Girl 6* (1996), Berry next agreed to a guest spot in the film-biz satire *Welcome to Hollywood* (1998). Written and directed by Tony Markes and Adam Rifkin, who also co-star, this is another 'mockumentary' which spoofs an easy target to moderate effect. Like *CB4*, *Welcome to Hollywood* gives real-life celebrities the chance to show they are good sports with a sense of humour. Rifkin plays a film director who follows aspiring young actor Markes around Hollywood as he tries to find that elusive big break. Berry appears as 'herself' along with Sandra Bullock, Nicolas Cage, Glenn Close, Cameron Diaz, Laurence Fishburne, Peter Fonda, Cuba Gooding Jr, Dennis Hopper, Will Smith, Jada Pinkett Smith, John Travolta and many more. *Welcome to Hollywood* received a limited theatrical release in Los Angeles, opening on 27 October 2000.

If Hollywood still seemed uncertain about Berry, she received star treatment on television. The producers of the hit sitcom *Frasier* came calling with another guest role. She supplied the voice of Betsy, one of Dr Frasier Crane's phone-in 'patients', in the episode 'Room Service', first broadcast on 3 March 1998.

Berry played a more substantial small screen role in the made-for-cable production *Introducing Dorothy Dandridge* (1999). Berry had long wanted to make a biopic of tragic star Dorothy Dandridge (1922-65), the first African-American to be nominated for a Best Actress Academy Award. Born in the same Cleveland hospital as Berry, Dandridge was also light-skinned, partly due to her mixed-race ancestry. Berry closely identified with Dandridge, who'd endured many of the same traumas: a broken family, abusive relationships, failed marriages, an estranged sister, career setbacks and the ever-present racial discrimination.

Berry had another, equally personal reason for making the film. Up until now, none of her starring roles had really tested her ability as a dramatic actress. Berry felt that some Hollywood insiders regarded her as just another ex-beauty queen and model who got lucky. There were even vicious rumours that she'd used her looks to advance her career via the casting couch.

Competition for the role of Dorothy Dandridge was intense, with singers-turned-actresses Diana Ross and Whitney Houston both expressing a strong interest. When Berry finally won out, she believed it was meant to be, telling Bob Thompson: "I got it because I think I'm probably the most passionate about it … I feel that Dorothy Dandridge passed me the ball, because our lives were so alike."

Best known for playing the sensual, outgoing and promiscuous *Carmen Jones* (1954), Dandridge was herself shy and fiercely moral. Brought up by her mother, actress Ruby Dandridge, Dorothy knew little of her father Cyril, who abandoned the family before she

was born. Dorothy didn't encounter Cyril until the early 1950s, when he revealed that she had a white grandparent. Father and daughter never met again.

Dorothy had an older sister, Vivian, with whom she performed professionally as 'The Wonderful Children'. On stage from the age of four, Dorothy enjoyed some success as a child actress. Ruby Dandridge took her daughters to Los Angeles, where Dorothy appeared in the Marx Brothers comedy *A Day at the Races* (1937). In *Sun Valley Serenade* (1941), a vehicle for skating star Sonja Henie, Dorothy took part in a musical number with dancer Harold Nicholas, her then boyfriend, and his brother Fayard. It's notable that their spirited song-and-dance rendition of 'Chattanooga Choo-Choo' was designed to be easily cut from the film, leaving no obvious gap. Production company Twentieth Century-Fox would then have a whites-only version of the movie for its Deep South distributors.

Dandridge finally played a dramatic film role in *The Bright Road* (1953). Produced by MGM, this above-average 'B' feature cast her as an idealistic schoolteacher opposite leading man Harry Belafonte, making his film debut. Dandridge returned to Fox for her best-known film, the lavish Cinemascope musical *Carmen Jones* (1954). Dandridge fought hard to win the title role, one of the few lead parts in 1950s Hollywood films that only a black actress could play. Produced and directed by Otto Preminger, the movie was based on a hit Broadway update of Georges Bizet's *Carmen*, with new lyrics by Oscar Hammerstein II. Dandridge led the all-black cast alongside the better-known Harry Belafonte, her *Bright Road* co-star.

Shooting *Carmen Jones* proved a tough experience for Dandridge, both

ABOVE:
Introducing Dorothy Dandridge. Otto Preminger (Klaus Maria Brandauer) directs Dorothy Dandridge during the filming of *Carmen Jones*.

LEFT:
Introducing Dorothy Dandridge. Dorothy Dandridge (Halle Berry) – Hollywood's first African-American leading lady?

on a professional and personal level. A perfectionist tormented by self-doubt, she worried that she would fail in the film, her one shot at Hollywood stardom. Preminger, who had a 'fascination' with black women, began an affair with Dandridge, nearly 20 years his junior. This short-lived relationship did not make things any easier for the star. Despite Dandridge's proven singing talent, her vocals were dubbed by opera student Marilyn Horne. In fairness to Preminger and Fox, *Carmen Jones'* score was extremely demanding, far beyond Dandridge's nightclub experience. Co-star Harry Belafonte, a gifted calypso singer, was also dubbed, by LeVerne Hutchersen. This compromise didn't prevent Dandridge from being Oscar-nominated for her passionate performance. She lost out to Grace Kelly, who took home the Best Actress award for *The Country Girl* (1954). An aristocratic WASP from a wealthy family, Kelly could not have been more different.

Short of roles for their new 'coloured' stars, Fox cast Dandridge and Belafonte in *Island in the Sun* (1957) alongside James Mason, Joan Fontaine and Joan Collins. Dandridge reunited with ex-lover Otto Preminger for *Porgy and Bess* (1959). Based on the successful opera, with lyrics by DuBose Heyward and music by George Gershwin, this saga of Catfish Row paired Dandridge's fallen woman with Sidney Poitier's beggar. This time around, Dandridge's singing was dubbed by Adele Addison. *Porgy and Bess* did not repeat *Carmen Jones'* success, marking the end of Dandridge's career in major American movies. Her last film was the British-produced *Moment of Danger* (1960), which sank without trace. A few years later, Dandridge declared bankruptcy.

After years of false starts and network indifference, *Introducing Dorothy Dandridge* finally got a greenlight from Home Box Office. The HBO deal involved Esparza and Katz Productions, with Moctesuma Esparza, Robert Katz and Halle Berry serving as co-executive producers. Budgeted at $8 million, *Introducing Dorothy Dandridge* was a major undertaking for all concerned. Looking for a sympathetic director, Berry hired Martha Coolidge. Aside from the teen comedy-fantasy *Real Genius* (1985), starring a young Val Kilmer, Coolidge specialised in serious, character-driven films like *Rambling Rose* (1991), for which mother-and-daughter stars Diane Ladd and Laura Dern both earned Academy Award nominations, and *Angie* (1994), starring Geena Davis as a pregnant single woman in search of a more fulfilling life.

Berry's singing had been dubbed for *Why Do Fools Fall in Love*. Determined to make the role of Dorothy Dandridge entirely her own, Berry did not want a voice double for the musical sequences. In the event, Berry realised she couldn't match Dandridge's vocal range and hired Wendi Williams to cover most of the songs. A scene recreating *Carmen Jones* used the original Marilyn Horne recording.

Introducing Dorothy Dandridge is based on a book by Earl Mills, Dandridge's white manager, who stuck with her throughout a turbulent career. The script was co-written by Scott Abbott and Shonda Rhimes, a largely untested talent. Two years earlier, Rhimes had scripted and directed a short film, *Blossoms and Veils* (1997), starring well-known black actors Jada Pinkett Smith, Omar Epps and C C H Pounder. For the score, Berry and her fellow producers hired veteran composer Elmer Bernstein, forever associated with *The Magnificent Seven* (1960).

The strong supporting cast was led by Loretta Devine, cast as mother Ruby Dandridge. Devine's film credits included *Waiting to Exhale* (1995), a hit tale of black girlfriends looking for love in the upmarket 'hood. The role of sister Vivian Dandridge went to Cynda Williams, who'd played a supporting role in Spike Lee's *Mo' Better Blues* (1990). Williams previously worked with Berry on *The Wedding*, another upmarket television production. Obba Babatunde, who played first husband Harold Nicholas, had appeared in *The Silence of the Lambs* (1991) and the Eddie Murphy-Martin Lawrence hit *Life* (1999).

The pivotal role of Earl Mills went to Brent Spiner, best known as loveable android Data in *Star Trek: The Next Generation* (1987-1994) and its film spin-offs. The Austrian director Otto Preminger was played by Klaus Maria Brandauer. Acclaimed for his dazzling performance in the Hungarian film *Mephisto* (1982), Brandauer had subsequently appeared in the James Bond movie *Never Say Never Again* (1983) and *Out of Africa* (1985), for which he received an Academy Award nomination.

Having done extensive research into Dandridge's life, Berry knew that portraying her on film would be an emotionally gruelling experience. As she explained:

> You have to find a way to be sad on every day, in every scene, in every moment. And always try to hide the sadness. And you'll get the essence of who she was.

On a lighter note, Berry found herself drawn to the styles of the 1950s and 1960s, telling Tyler McLeod: "I loved the whole period: The clothes, the hairdos … I wish I was alive in the 50s." If Berry *had* been a contemporary of Dorothy Dandridge, however, she probably wouldn't have fared much better.

As a personal homage to a great fallen star, *Introducing Dorothy Dandridge* is a triumph for Halle Berry. As a piece of television drama, it falls short. The film begins in 1965 on the day of Dandridge's death. Talking to an old friend on the phone, Dandridge assembles a photo-collage of her life and career. It's not the most subtle narrative device and hints at the film's structural problems.

The story jumps back ten years to 1955 and the night of the Academy Award ceremony. We then travel to 1940 and Dandridge's time at Harlem's famous Cotton Club in New York City. Here, she meets future husband Harold Nicholas, a gifted dancer and notorious womaniser. Admitting that Nicholas is a father substitute, Dandridge soon realises he is no more dependable. Their daughter Harolyn, born in 1943, proves to be brain-damaged, owing to a lack of oxygen during delivery. Dorothy blames herself for this tragedy, heartbroken that Harolyn can never call her 'Mother'.

Divorcing Nicholas in the late 1940s, Dandridge marries restaurateur Jack Denison, a white man, in 1959. Social prejudice aside, the union proves a costly mistake, lasting a painful three years. Drunken, dishonest and violent, Denison beats Dorothy up for merely suggesting that he get dressed. Up until *Carmen Jones*, Dandridge's most prominent movie role is in RKO's *Tarzan's Peril* (1951), cast opposite Lex Barker as a sultry jungle princess. Feeling that Dandridge doesn't look African enough, the producers darken her skin for the film. She enjoys more success as a nightclub singer, commanding a fee of $3500 a week.

Having beaten Lena Horne and Eartha Kitt to the title role of *Carmen Jones*, Dandridge seems to have it made in Hollywood for a short time. Supported by co-stars Harry Belafonte (Andre Carthen) and Sidney Poitier (Ben Brown), she discovers that the white men in her life are not so reliable. Darryl F. Zanuck (William Atherton), the boss at Twentieth Century-Fox, promises her stardom, while lover Otto Preminger hints at marriage "…when the time is right". After Dandridge rejects a role in *The King and I* (1956) on the grounds that she won't play a slave, Zanuck loses interest in her. Preminger, who appears to really love Dandridge, will not risk his career and social status for one woman.

The film omits at least one major episode from Dandridge's life. During the late 1950s, she successfully sued *Confidential* magazine, a notorious celebrity scandal sheet, for an article that claimed to reveal intimate details of her sex life. Sadly, this minor victory did little for her Hollywood standing. Elsewhere, *Introducing Dorothy Dandridge* doesn't flinch from portraying the more shocking aspects of its subject's life. Dorothy is sexually abused by her mother's female lover, 'Auntie', who performs a 'virginity check' after the first date with Harold Nicholas. This attack leaves her sexually frigid, frustrating Nicholas on their wedding night. Director Martha Coolidge, who was raped as a teenager, knows about abuse and suffering at first hand, and these scenes are painful to watch.

Introducing Dorothy Dandridge continues on its gloomy path. Dandridge's career troubles and messy divorce from Denison in 1962 lead to alcoholism, prescription drug abuse

and bankruptcy. Dandridge seems on the verge of a minor comeback, both on stage and in movies, when she dies, aged only 42, from an overdose of Tofranil, an anti-depressant. While the Los Angeles coroner records an open verdict, Dorothy Dandridge is widely believed to have committed suicide.

Though Berry pulls out all the stops, *Introducing Dorothy Dandridge* suffers from a truncated narrative, insubstantial supporting characters and numerous showbiz clichés. Cameo appearances from 'Marilyn Monroe' and 'Ava Gardner' are both pointless and distracting. The Jack Denison marriage is dealt with in a few short scenes, leaving the impression that Dandridge recklessly ignored her family's advice, drawn to a man she knew to be dangerous.

In the title role, Berry works hard to capture Dandridge's star quality. Lip-synching aside, Berry handles the musical numbers with assurance. The script is less successful, resorting to soap opera dramatics. Early on in the film, Dorothy proclaims: "I'm staying young and beautiful till the day I die," a touch of heavy dramatic irony. Her crucial relationship with Earl Mills is mishandled, partly due to the miscasting of Brent Spiner. First introduced to Dandridge underneath a piano, Mills declares: "You've got a face like an angel, you know that?" Mills' unrequited love for Dorothy is both predictable and unaffecting.

The film deals effectively with the ever-present racial divide. Performing in a Miami nightclub, Dandridge is barred from using the whites-only bathrooms, pissing into a paper cup instead. Ready to quit, she berates the manager, only to learn that not all white Southerners are racists. Determined not to be beaten, Dandridge wins over the hostile crowd. As the star turn in Las Vegas, Dandridge can't swim in the hotel pool. Defiantly dipping a toe in the water, she later finds that the pool has been drained and scrubbed by black workers. The sight of Dandridge's naked corpse, face down on her bathroom floor, is unsettling, though largely for Berry's willingness to appear so vulnerable on screen.

Having proved herself as Hollywood's first black leading lady, Dandridge found that the movie industry had no place for her. Thwarted throughout her short life by America's ingrained racism, Dandridge made her feelings clear: "It's such a waste. It makes you half alive. It gives you nothing. It takes away." Faced with the same prejudice 30 years on, Halle Berry could appreciate the sentiment.

Introducing Dorothy Dandridge received its world premiere on 14 August 1999 in Dandridge's, and Halle Berry's, home town of Cleveland, Ohio. Advertised with the tagline 'She was everything America wanted a movie star to be… except white', the film made its television debut on 21 August. In Britain, it received a video and DVD release as *Face of an Angel*, after Earl Mills' nickname for Dandridge. Presumably, the distributors felt that Dandridge's real name meant little to UK viewers.

Critics previously unconvinced of Berry's dramatic depth changed their minds. Her committed, gutsy performance won a deserved Emmy Award for Outstanding Lead Actress in a Miniseries or Movie. The Emmys are American television's equivalent of the Academy Awards, and carry a similar weight. As one of *Introducing Dorothy Dandridge*'s executive producers, Berry also shared an Emmy nomination for Outstanding Made for Television Movie. The film won further Emmys for art direction, cinematography, costumes and hair styling.

Berry also picked up a Screen Actors Guild award for Outstanding Performance by a Female Actor in a Television Movie or Miniseries as well as the Golden Globe award for Best Performance by an Actress in a Mini-Series or Motion Picture Made for TV. Handed out by Hollywood's Foreign Press Association, the once-despised Golden Globes now carry a certain prestige. Berry's guest of honour at the Golden Globes ceremony was Yvonne Sims, her former guidance counsellor. Nominated for a Golden Satellite Award, Berry won Outstanding Actress at the Image Awards, which declared *Introducing Dorothy Dandridge* the Outstanding TV movie/Miniseries/Dramatic Special. The Image Awards also handed Berry a Special Award for Entertainer of the Year.

Awards aside, *Introducing Dorothy Dandridge* finally convinced Halle Berry that she had the talent, and determination, to pursue the top film roles on equal terms with other leading actresses: Interviewed by Robin Taylor, she explained:

I had to prove that I was more than a model and that role freed me up to do things I'd always wanted to do. Without Dorothy behind me I'm not sure I'd have had the courage to go after *Monster's Ball*.

RIGHT:

Halle attends the premiere of *Introducing Dorothy Dandridge*, held in Cleveland, Ohio.

X-RATED

AS *Bulworth* faded from Hollywood executives' minds, Halle Berry found that getting decent film roles was still an uphill struggle, despite her success in *Introducing Dorothy Dandridge*. Twentieth Century Fox, the studio behind *Bulworth*, offered Berry a co-starring role in *X-Men* (2000). Based on the popular Marvel comic book, this $75 million production would prove one of the strongest superhero movies. Berry accepted the fourth-billed part of Ororo Munroe, better known as Storm. One of the few black superheroes, Storm offered comic fans a positive, if otherworldly, role model.

Whatever the limitations of the format, *X-Men* boasted a top director in the shape of Bryan Singer, whose career had taken off with *The Usual Suspects* (1995), an ingenious, if tricksy, thriller starring Gabriel Bryne and Kevin Spacey. Singer made a deal with Hollywood major Columbia TriStar for his eagerly awaited follow-up movie, *Apt Pupil* (1997). Based on a Stephen King novella, the film stars Brad Renfro as a high school student who forges an unhealthy – and unholy – bond with fugitive Nazi war criminal Ian McKellen. Too dark for mainstream tastes, *Apt Pupil* met with mixed reviews and little box-office business.

Singer devised the story for *X-Men* with Tom De Santo, one of the co-producers on *Apt Pupil*. The actual screenplay was written by newcomer David Hayter, with a little uncredited help from a pool of script doctors that included Singer's old associate Christopher McQuarrie and Joss Whedon, the man behind *Buffy the Vampire Slayer*.

X-Men attracted a strong cast led by British actor Patrick Stewart, best known for playing Captain Jean-Luc Picard in *Star Trek: The Next Generation*. Stewart was perfect casting for Professor Xavier, the genius behind the X-Men, while the role of chief villain Magneto went to Ian McKellen, one of Britain's leading theatre actors who had resisted the Hollywood dollar for much of his career. Though McKellen had considered his ex-Nazi character in *Apt Pupil* too one-dimensional, he nevertheless signed up to play a costumed supervillain in a comic-book movie. Ironically, Magneto is revealed as a childhood victim of the Nazis.

Professor Xavier's X-Men were played by relative unknowns, which at least kept the budget down. Bryan Singer and Twentieth Century Fox cast British actor Dougray Scott in the central role of Wolverine. Scott had worked his way up from Britflicks such as *Twin Town* (1997) and had already signed on to play a villain in the Tom Cruise production *Mission: Impossible 2* (2000), directed by Hong Kong action maestro John Woo. The part of Jean Grey, a telekinetic mind-reader, went to Famke Janssen, best known for *GoldenEye* (1995), the first James Bond film starring Pierce Brosnan. James Marsden played Scott Summers, aka Cyclops, Jean Grey's colleague and boyfriend. New Zealander Anna Paquin took the part of troubled teen mutant Rogue. As a child, Paquin had won a Best Supporting Actress Academy Award for her performance in Jane Campion's *The Piano* (1993). The script originally included a fifth X-Man,

The Beast. Bryan Singer had to drop the character when Fox objected to the cost of the special make-up work involved.

Bruce Davison, who had appeared in *Apt Pupil*, was cast as a bigoted politician on an anti-mutant crusade. Ian McKellen's fellow bad guys included actor-stuntman Ray Park, cast as the unlovely Toad. No stranger to comic-book fantasy, Park had played the aggressive, if taciturn, villain Darth Maul in *Star Wars: Episode I The Phantom Menace* (1999). Park had even less opportunity to converse in Tim Burton's *Sleepy Hollow* (1999), doubling for Christopher Walken as the Headless Horseman.

Having proved herself as a 'legitimate' dramatic actress with *Introducing Dorothy Dandridge*, Berry now felt secure enough to take on a comic-book movie: "I would have felt that it was too risky for me before. Maybe a little too frivolous for a former model turned actress." A fan of both *The Usual Suspects* and *Apt Pupil*, Berry was confident that Bryan Singer would deliver a strong movie. Respected actors Stewart, McKellen and Paquin were all signed up for the film before Berry, which gave her another incentive to come on board. As Berry later admitted to *Toronto Sun* reporter Bob Thompson, she was not a big *X-Men* fan:

> When I finally got it, I was embarrassed to say I didn't know much about *X-Men*, but then I found out that nobody else in the cast did either … I have heard that Storm's one of the most beloved characters. I feel the pressure. I hope I can do her justice.

Marvel Comics' *X-Men* had been going since 1964, the original line-up consisting of Cyclops, Marvel Girl aka Jean Grey, Iceman, Angel and The Beast. In 1974, 94 issues later, most of the team were replaced, leaving Cyclops paired with Nightcrawler, Colossus, Banshee, Thunderbird, Wolverine and Storm. Marvel Girl later made a comeback, replacing the deceased Thunderbird. By the late 1990s, *X-Men* was the world's bestselling comic book.

The film version needed to win the fans' approval to be a hit. While Fox had Marvel supremo Stan Lee on board for the production, this didn't guarantee a successful movie. Negative word-of-mouth could kill the film stone dead. Rising star Freddie Prinze Jr, a big *X-Men* fan, turned down the role of Cyclops, believing the film couldn't do justice to the original comic book. A few years later, Prinze agreed to co-star in the big screen, live-action version of *Scooby Doo* (2002).

Originally set for the Christmas season, *X-Men*'s release date was brought forward six months to summer 2000, giving director Bryan Singer a tight production schedule. Most of *X-Men* was filmed in and around Toronto, Canada, with some additional location work back in New York City. Production began in September 1999, lasting until February 2000. Having grown up in Cleveland, on Lake Erie, Berry had no difficulties with the freezing Canadian winter weather.

Three weeks into the *X-Men* shoot, Twentieth Century Fox discovered it had a serious problem. Paramount's *Mission: Impossible 2* had fallen behind schedule, including scenes requiring Dougray Scott. Unable to make his start date on *X-Men*, Scott withdrew from the film. Already under pressure, Singer petitioned to have the production put on hold, buying himself more time. Committed to a summer 2000 release,

RIGHT:
Halle looking cool at the *X-Men* premiere.

62

Fox refused to halt filming. The studio had to find a new Wolverine in a hurry. Going back to their original shortlist, the producers decided that Australian actor Hugh Jackman seemed a good bet. Jackman flew to *X-Men*'s Toronto location and auditioned for the role on the spot. For his screen test, Jackman and Anna Paquin acted out the first scene between Wolverine and Rogue. Singer liked what he saw and *X-Men* had a new recruit.

Berry had her own problems during filming. Storm's eyes were supposed to glow white when she used her powers. Singer wanted to achieve this effect with opaque contact lenses, specially designed for the character. Berry found the lenses too uncomfortable to wear, even for short periods of time. In the end, the effect was added during post-production with CGI trickery. Looking back on the shoot two years later, Singer did not gloss over the production traumas: "I've developed very thick skin now … it's all uphill from that *X-Men* experience."

Beneath the hi-tech hardware, heavy-duty action and unlikely costumes, *X-Men* the movie is an allegory about difference, alienation and prejudice. To underline this point, the film opens in 1944 Poland as German troops herd Jewish prisoners into a concentration camp. While the rain beats down on this oppressive blue-grey landscape, the young Magneto is forcibly separated from his parents. Fast-forward to the new millennium, and the US government debates compulsory mutant registration. X-Men guru Professor Xavier believes in peaceful co-habitation between humans and mutants. His former friend Magneto favours all-out war, forcibly turning humans into new strains of mutant.

The original *X-Men* comic attributed its heroes' mutation to atmospheric radiation. Moving with the times, the film switches to genetic mutation, which tends to kick in with puberty. The plot centres on Rogue and Wolverine as they are introduced to Professor Xavier's special school. Rogue absorbs the life force of anyone she touches, which makes personal relationships difficult. Wolverine boasts amazing regenerative powers, rendering him a natural fighter. A victim of surgical tampering, he also has a metal alloy-enhanced skeleton, with razor-sharp claws.

X-Men is a well-crafted film, with assured direction, impressive set designs and well-achieved CGI effects. Twenty minutes in, Berry makes her first appearance as cloaked superhero Storm, described by *Guardian* journalist Paul Howlett as "a sort of weathergirl with attitude". Distinguished by her long white-blonde hair, glowing eyes and nifty dark blue outfit, Storm thwarts evil mutant Sabertooth (Tyler Mane) with an instant blizzard.

One of Xavier's first students, she now teaches at his academy. Creating lightning bolts and sea mist, Storm seems rather passive in herself, rooted to the spot while her meteorological powers rage around her. In contrast to her name, Storm serves as a harmonious, calming influence. Transformed by Magneto into an ersatz mutant, the bigoted Senator Kelly (Davison) begs Xavier for help. Discussing the mutual distrust between them, Storm tells Kelly about her feelings towards humans: "…I'm scared of them". She also witnesses his messy, watery death, proof that Magento's 'treatment' is unstable.

Aside from a running battle with Sabertooth, Storm doesn't have enough to do, often just standing in the background, looking concerned. She plays no part in the tense triangle that develops between Wolverine, Jean Grey and Cyclops, remaining detached. In the *X-Men* comic book, Storm is a *bona fide* African goddess, something omitted from the finished film. Pushed for time in post-production, Singer cut a flashback scene, set in Africa, where the young Storm drops hailstones on a gang of bullies.

A number of Berry's other scenes were cut down to tighten the film's pace. In one trimmed sequence, Storm teaches a history class. Drawing an obvious parallel between mutants and the early Christians, she points out that the Roman persecution of the latter ended when the Emperor Constantine converted to the new faith. Intentionally or not, this seems to endorse Magneto's campaign of mass genetic reprogramming. Another cut scene features an after-class discussion between Storm and Rogue, touching on Wolverine, the school, Professor Xavier and the impossibility of a cure for Rogue's condition.

X-Men's scrappy finale is set inside and on top of the Statue of Liberty, which tends to cramp the action. Battling Toad among the tacky souvenirs, Storm is kicked down an elevator shaft. Down but not out, she retaliates with a lighting strike that blasts the slimy fiend into the sea.

Advertised with the tagline 'Protecting Those Who Fear Them', *X-Men* opened in the United States on 14 July 2000, grossing an impressive $157.3 million. The film hit British cinemas a month later, on 18 August, taking £14.88 million at the box-office. Halle Berry, Hugh Jackman, James Marsden and Anna Paquin shared a 2001 MTV Movie Award nomination for Best On-Screen Team.

If *X-Men* was Halle Berry's big success of 2000, she experienced a major low the same year. On the night of 23 February, Berry was driving through the Sunset Boulevard district of Los Angeles in a rented Chevrolet Blazer. For whatever reason, she jumped a red light and hit another car. The collision left Berry with a gash in her head which required 20 stitches. The other driver, Hetal Raythatha, suffered a broken wrist. Berry drove away before the authorities arrived, seeking treatment at a nearby hospital, where she reported the incident to a police officer. This left her in an awkward legal position, as the offence of reckless driving carried a possible three-year prison sentence.

On 10 May, in an LA Superior Court, Berry pleaded no contest to a misdemeanour charge of leaving the scene of a traffic accident. She was fined $13,500, placed on three years' unsupervised probation, and ordered to carry out 200 hours of community service. Hetal Raythatha brought a civil action against Berry, which was quickly settled.

Faced with a barrage of bad publicity and media criticism, Berry refused to be crushed. Accepting the law's punishment for her misdemeanour, she had no time for the judgment of others, telling Libby Brooks: "I'm not perfect, I'm not without flaws … but I'm confident in who I am." Berry claims that the incident actually strengthened her character: "That was the start of being released from that need to be liked. I learned to get a thicker skin." One consequence of this new resolve was a determination to take riskier roles.

Throughout the whole episode, boyfriend Eric Benet remained a constant source of support. After two

good years with Benet, Berry decided that she'd met "the love of my life". Admitting that Benet was something of a father figure for her, Berry also praised him for accepting her faults and mistakes. Previous lovers were only interested in her looks, refusing to acknowledge the woman underneath.

Berry and Benet had become engaged on 14 August 1999, six months before her car accident. On 24 January 2001, they were married in a secret beach ceremony. The location of the wedding was not disclosed at first, though both California and Mexico were suggested, and the happy couple did not go public on their union for three months. A year later, Berry confirmed that the marriage took place in Los Angeles. For their honeymoon, Berry and Benet spent two weeks on an island in the Maldives, near India.

According to *The National Enquirer*, Berry did not embark on her second marriage without laying down one strict condition. If Benet ever proved unfaithful, he'd lose Berry, his LA-based career and any children they had, walking away with nothing. Apparently, Benet made a solemn vow of fidelity. Regarded as something of a ladies' man, Benet was soon rumoured to have broken his promise on at least one occasion. Berry fiercely denied these stories, claiming that the marriage was strong: "Eric's very supportive of what I'm trying to do as an actress and a black woman." An aspiring actor himself, Benet played a small role in the Mariah Carey vehicle *Glitter* (2001), which unfortunately proved a champion turkey.

Berry also had a good relationship with Benet's daughter, India, who seemed unfazed by her stepmother's ever-growing celebrity. As Berry explained to Robin Taylor: "Having two parents in the entertainment industry, she's very mature about the whole thing, it's no big deal for her."

ABOVE:
Halle with her fiance Eric Benet in 1999.

Unwilling to disrupt India's education, Berry wouldn't take her on film locations for long periods, telling David A Keeps: "When I'm working she comes to visit or I go home ... we talk a lot and stay connected."

Berry's car accident came around the time she decided not to reunite with *Boomerang* star Eddie Murphy. Apparently, Berry had agreed to appear opposite former lover Murphy in *The Adventures of Pluto Nash* (2002), a science fiction comedy set on the moon. The director was Ron Underwood and the supporting cast included blaxploitation icon Pam Grier and Peter Boyle, who later worked with Berry on *Monster's Ball*. According to *The Hollywood Reporter*, Berry dropped out of the film just a few weeks before production started, on 10 April 2000. Her publicist denied that Berry's recent traffic accident played a part in this decision.

Murphy replaced Berry with Rosario Dawson, who co-starred in *Josie and the Pussycats* (2001) and went on to make *Men in Black II* (2002). Like Berry, Dawson found an early career break with writer-director Spike Lee, appearing in *He Got Game* (1998), her third movie. Born in 1979, Dawson bears a passing resemblance to Berry, ten years her senior. Unable to get his first choice of leading lady, Murphy had clearly settled for a younger model. *The Adventures of Pluto Nash* didn't reach US cinemas until 16 August 2002, two years after filming wrapped.

Fourth billed on *X-Men*, Berry moved up a place for *Swordfish* (2001), the film which first acquainted paying audiences with her nipples. Five years on from *Executive Decision*, Berry reunited with producer Joel Silver for this contrived, self-conscious thriller. Silver and Warner Bros agreed to pay Berry a respectable $2.5 million, still less than her asking price.

BELOW:
Swordfish. Having a laugh with John Travolta

Swordfish also reunited Berry with *X-Men* co-star Hugh Jackman, now a rising Hollywood player in his own right. The movie's big star turn came in the bulky form of John Travolta, who beat John Cusack and Val Kilmer to the role of master criminal Gabriel Shear. The supporting cast included gifted black actor Don Cheadle, who'd appeared in *Bulworth*, and former footballer Vinnie Jones, the self-styled bad boy of English soccer. Three years earlier, Jones had made a passable film debut in the 'mockney' crime comedy *Lock, Stock and Two Smoking Barrels* (1998); his convincing turn as a thuggish debt collector with a line in dry quips drew Hollywood interest.

Swordfish was directed by Dominic Sena, a former pop video specialist whose credits included Janet Jackson's 'Rhythm Nation 1814' (1989). Sena first came to notice with *Kalifornia* (1993), starring Brad Pitt, Juliette Lewis and *X-Files* mainstay David Duchovny. A self-referential serial killer thriller, *Kalifornia* was followed by *Gone in 60 Seconds* (2000), starring Nicolas Cage as the world's greatest car thief and featuring Vinnie Jones in his Hollywood debut. When Silver suggested Halle Berry for *Swordfish*, Sena was immediately taken with her 'cosmopolitan' quality: "a great global babe". *Swordfish* screenwriter Skip Woods had only one previous film

ABOVE:
Swordfish. Halle relaxes between takes with co-star Hugh Jackman.

credit, having written and directed the crime thriller *Thursday* (1998). He took *Swordfish*'s title from the Marx Brothers comedy *Horse Feathers* (1932), where 'swordfish' is a speakeasy password.

Budgeted at $80 million, *Swordfish* began shooting on 19 October 2000. The sunny locations included Los Angeles and Nice, standing in for Monte Carlo. According to Sena, the production had a good working atmosphere, Travolta and Jackman getting on particularly well. Described by Sena as "pretty ballsy", Berry declined a crash mat for a scene where her character is pushed from a trailer. Indulging in on-set group hugs, Berry seemed to have a good time: "It's kind of a fun ride," she said. Co-star Don Cheadle had the best perspective on the movie: "It's like being a big kid with the best toys."

But, even by hi-tech action movie standards, *Swordfish* has little going for it. In the first scene, Gabriel Shear comes out with ill-advised line: "You know what the problem with Hollywood is? They make shit." Sena's tricksy direction is restless and fidgety, generating minimal tension. Employing the old flashback device, Woods' smart-ass, self-referential script cannot hide several gaping plot holes and a general lack of ideas.

An international man of mystery, Gabriel hangs out with Ginger Knowles (Berry), his accomplice and lover. For their latest $9.5 billion scam, they require the services of ex-con Stanley Jobson (Jackman), an expert computer hacker who ran into trouble with the FBI. Forbidden to touch a keyboard, Stanley now greases oil pumps in Texas. It's an honest job. A broken man, Stanley lost custody of his young daughter to his ex-wife, now a drunken porn star. Rampant misogyny aside, this gives him an honourable motive to

join with Gabriel, earning the money he needs for an expensive court case. Held at gunpoint, Stanley must prove himself by breaking a government access code in 60 seconds while receiving oral sex. According to Sena, producer Joel Silver felt the blowjob was vital to the plot. Without his Wolverine hairstyle and sideburns, Jackman looks like a more macho version of Rupert Everett. Still, the single ear-ring is a bold touch.

The far from angelic Gabriel sports an unflattering goatee and some top-ranking political connections. An expert in counter-terrorism, he knows all the moves and most of the right (or wrong) people. Respected playwright and actor Sam Shepard turns up as a corrupt senator, announcing: "Someone's cock's liable to wind up on the block on this one and I guarantee it won't be mine." It's a safe bet Shepard didn't write this line himself. Cast as Marco, Gabriel's top henchman, Vinnie Jones waves a gun with conviction but still can't handle dialogue.

Filled with the usual car chases and explosions, *Swordfish* also offers a bus towed by a helicopter through Los Angeles' skyscrapers. As with Joel Silver's earlier *Executive Decision*, *Swordfish* makes for a strangely discomfiting viewing experience in the light of 11 September 2001. It seems that Gabriel is really an ultra-patriot who plans, finances and executes counter-strikes against terrorist states. Gabriel even gets the line: "Our job is to make terrorism so horrific that it becomes unthinkable to attack Americans."

While *The X-Men* at least gave Berry a piece of the action, she's largely wasted in *Swordfish*. First seen in a red hot sports car and matching mini-dress, Ginger is a top golfer, giving Stanley – and audiences – a good view of her rear as she takes a shot. That said, she's no easy lay: "I'm not here to suck your dick, Stanley." This initial encounter originally played a lot longer, filled with heavy-duty double entendres. Anxious to keep the story moving, Sena and Silver drastically cut the sequence to its bare essentials. Incidentally, Berry had never held a golf club before shooting the scene, her swing leaving something to be desired.

Another scene featuring Berry and Jackman suffers from awkward post-production rewriting and dubbing, as the original dialogue didn't play well. But, comfortably cast as a sensuous, seductive and extremely bright woman, Berry handles the extensive computer jargon with assurance.

Berry's best-known scene in *Swordfish* involves Ginger indulging in topless book reading. Looking relaxed on a sunbed, Ginger seems amused when she lifts the book from her chest and Stanley jumps several miles. For the record, this brief nudity is in a non-sexual context, with Stanley disconcerted rather than aroused. Berry supposedly charged Joel Silver an extra $500,000 for baring her breasts, seen in two brief shots. Berry dismissed this rumour as nonsense, arguing: "I would sell these babies for way more money than that." What she didn't deny was the gratuitous titillation of the scene: "…I didn't need to be naked. It was my choice." Having remained fully clothed, more or less, in her previous outings for Silver, Berry obviously felt that the time had come: "I've never really explored that part of myself on screen before."

In HBO's *The Making of Swordfish*, Berry admitted to pre-filming nerves: "The nudity thing scared me to death." Joel Silver confirmed Berry's version of events: "There was never a discussion about it. It's crazy. The role was

scripted as is … Can you imagine negotiating that?" In the HBO documentary/plug, Silver is heard to say: "You're never going to worry about that again." Berry responds: "…every day for the rest of my life…" Presumably, she's joking.

On the other hand, co-producer Jonathan Krane publicly stated that Berry was paid extra to go topless. In an unusually frank interview, Krane claimed that he hadn't wanted any nudity in the film and hoped Berry would refuse to strip: "A lot of actresses turned it down on the basis of that, and they should. I didn't think it was necessary in the movie." Questioned at a *Swordfish* press conference, Krane went further: "I don't like it. I've made 43 films that I have produced and I don't think I've had a naked girl in any of them until this." Director Dominic Sena, who also shot a bikini top version of the scene for television prints, remained diplomatic: "I think Halle was fine with doing the nudity."

Throughout *Swordfish*, the script plays with the idea that Ginger is some kind of double agent. Early on, she tells Stanley: "I'm not what you think I am." When Stanley finds Ginger dressed only in black underwear and a secret recording device, she admits to being an undercover DEA operative. She certainly packs a heavy-duty firearm. As Sena put it: "Underwear and guns. That's a good combination."

Offscreen for most of *Swordfish*'s protracted finale, Ginger gets strung up by Gabriel's men, her cover blown. Given 60 seconds to save her life, Stanley sees Ginger gunned down by Gabriel. In a double twist, it's revealed that Gabriel and Ginger staged her 'execution'. Far from being a dead DEA agent, Ginger is alive and well with Gabriel in Monte Carlo. Modelling new

nudity." Berry felt she needed to re-evaluate her attitude: "…I realised I was allowing what people thought of me to stop me." As Berry explained to *Glamour* reporter David A Keeps: "I wasn't afraid to take the role. Life is about taking risks … I just didn't go

into it worrying too much about what anyone was going to think." Berry certainly couldn't be accused of doing *Monster's Ball* for the money, earning just $100,000 for her role.

Budgeted at a mere $4 million, *Monster's Ball* was filmed on locations in the southern state of Louisiana. Director Marc Forster and his crew were permitted to shoot inside the State Prison in Angola. Despite the harrowing subject matter, the *Monster's Ball* production didn't leave the cast and crew emotional wrecks, largely thanks to Billy Bob Thornton's good humour. Interviewed by Davisdvd.com, Forster explained: "Even though it's a drama and it's often very intense, the scene on the set was very light and funny."

As *Monster's Ball* gets rolling, things in Georgia, Alabama, are heavy and grim. Condemned man Lawrence Musgrove has one last meeting with his estranged wife Leticia and their teenage son, Tyrell (Coronji Calhoun), who remembers nothing of his father's life outside prison. The title refers to Musgrove's last meal, the evening equivalent of a condemned man's hearty breakfast. Apparently, the term originated in England, which is nothing to boast about.

From the start, *Monster's Ball* has weaknesses, notably the contrived, 'Movie of the Week'-type plot. Forster's direction is sometimes self-conscious, striving too hard for effect. That said, the build-up to Lawrence Musgrove's date with the electric chair is well handled, Forster dwelling on the details of the procedure. Allowed little dignity in his final minutes on earth, Musgrove must endure a shaved head, a cut-off trouser leg and even incontinence pants; Hank Grotowski and his team like to keep their executions clean.

A large proportion of America's Death Row inmates are poor and black. Any movie that attempts to address this issue is worthwhile.

Monster's Ball is kept afloat by its two leading performances. No stranger to Deep South melodrama, Billy Bob Thornton gives Hank Grotowski an understated sadness. A repressed, racist loner, Hank is employed as a Corrections Officer by the Georgia Penitentiary Service. Emotionally frozen, his love life consists of joyless sex with the local whore, who also services the more enthusiastic Sonny. Father and son both favour the standing rear-entry position, uninterested in any pretence of intimacy. Hank seems to derive more pleasure from eating chocolate ice cream at the local diner, where Leticia Musgrove works.

Berry felt that Hank's bigotry had a simple explanation: "This film deals with the fact that people are racist because they are taught to be." The script bears this out to an extent. Hank's appalling father, Buck, is a Deep South, Kentucky Fried, redneck monster. Keeping a scrapbook of local executions, Buck insults Leticia's sexuality with talk of "nigger juice". At Sonny's miserable, sparsely attended funeral, Buck dismisses his dead grandson as "weak". That said, the ill-fated Sonny has black friends and a liberal attitude.

Monster's Ball piles on the suffering to a near-ludicrous degree. Hank's mother killed herself, his son killed himself and God only knows what became of his wife. Buck is suffering from both arthritis and emphysema. Hank spends a lot of time cleaning blood off chairs, handbags and car seats. On balance, he doesn't seem a great romantic prospect.

But, if Hank Grotowski's life looks grim, things are a whole lot worse for Leticia Musgrove. At the beginning of Monster's Ball, her husband has been on Death Row for 11 years. As a black cop killer in the Deep South, Lawrence Musgrove never stood a chance. Living in near poverty, Leticia can no longer keep up the payments on her house. Barely 13, the grossly overweight Tyrell is hooked on sweets and chocolate. Beating her son, a "fat little piggy", for his candy bar addiction, Leticia seems less perturbed by her own heavy drinking. Berry later claimed that Monster's Ball was the first time she hadn't recognised herself on screen. Shortly after Lawrence's execution, Tyrell is knocked down by a car during a vaguely symbolic torrential downpour. In the space of a few days, Leticia has lost her husband, her son and her house. Furthermore, her car is falling to bits and her poorly paid job looks precarious.

Initially, Hank and Leticia seem united by loss rather than love. Drunk and reckless, the grieving Leticia wants to feel good and Hank is willing to oblige. The script called for an 'animalistic' treatment of sex, without going into any detail. Forster left the two sex scenes until the last four days of filming. Having worked closely with Forster and his crew over the past weeks, both Berry and Thornton had confidence in their collaborators. They also felt comfortable with the characters. As Berry later explained: "…we just went for it".

Initially assuming his preferred rear-entry position, Hank turns Leticia to face him, wanting to make love rather than just get laid. During the second encounter, Hank performs cunnilingus on Leticia, the camera staying on her face as she reaches orgasm. Angela Bassett regarded these scenes with contempt. As she explained to *Newsweek*: "…it's such a stereotype about black women and sexuality." Berry argued that the sex scenes were vital to the film:

> The tabloids made a big deal about it, but in the movie it's a catalyst for a change that ultimately saves their lives.

She also liked the fact that Leticia and Hank are equally exposed, and vulnerable. In the event, neither scene required more than one take, for which Berry was grateful: "…you don't really want to have to go there that many times." Forster gave Berry final approval on the finished sequences, which she felt helped her performance. As Berry explained to Louis B Hobson: "Just knowing I had a veto freed me to go wherever we had to when we were filming." It's notable that the sex scenes are carefully framed and lit, with no full-frontal nudity.

Husband Eric Benet had no problem with the film's explicit sex. Nevertheless, Berry arranged for him to see an early screening of the finished film, before the press had a chance to quiz him. "I did it out of respect to him. I didn't want him to see it on premiere night and have some reporter go 'So…?'" According to Berry, Benet gave her performance his full approval, nudity and all, telling her: "I'm really proud of you. You took a risk … I hope you keep doing that."

Monster's Ball has an odd, low-key finale which leaves several major plot points unresolved. Admitting that she needs to be looked after, Leticia gains a boyfriend, a new car and a place to live. As many critics pointed out, this is not an equal partnership. Hank seems happy with the arrangement: "I think

we're gonna be alright." As the camera tilts up to the starlit sky, the film seems to be attempting an understated yet profound conclusion. For the record, Berry stands by the ending, arguing that Leticia acts out of choice, rather than need. Promoting *Monster's Ball* in Britain, Berry told Libby Brooks:

> She [Leticia] was a fighter and I think she would have survived without him. I liked the ending because the one thing it didn't do was put a Hollywood bow on it. They didn't run off and get married. She wasn't pregnant. It left them with as much hope as conflict, and it was left for the audience to decide what happens in the morning.

Whether or not this ambiguous finale works, it's hard to argue with Berry's take on the overall film: "The racial divide is insane and ridiculous. In this film those beliefs are challenged."

While director Marc Forster and his stars expected *Monster's Ball* to be controversial, they probably hadn't anticipated censorship problems. The Motion Picture Association of America (MPAA) demanded cuts to the sex scenes. *Monster's Ball* needed an 'R' rating (Restricted: children under 17 require accompanying parent or adult guardian) to achieve wide distribution. The MPAA felt that the original version merited an adults only 'NC17' rating, the commercial kiss of death for a small, independent movie. Even the big studios bowed to the ratings board. When Stanley Kubrick's last film, *Eyes Wide Shut* (1999), was classified 'NC17' for its orgy sequence, Warner Bros prepared a softened 'R' version for the North American market. Unhappy with the MPAA's decision, Berry went public over the issue:

In America people are happy to watch a film in which someone blows someone else's head off, but those same people have a problem watching the most natural thing in the world – people making love.

Thirty years earlier, rising star Jack Nicholson made exactly the same point. Some things don't change. Berry still argues that "…the nudity and the violent nature of the sex scenes were essential to the story." The uncut, unrated version of *Monster's Ball* was subsequently released on DVD, along with the Blockbuster-friendly 'R' version.

Monster's Ball premiered at the American Film Institute Film Festival on 11 November 2001. The film went on limited release in Los Angeles and New York on 26 December, which qualified it for 2002 Academy Award consideration. *Monster's Ball* finally opened nationwide on 8 February 2002, eventually grossing a respectable $31.25 million. Many found Berry's raw, uninhibited performance astonishing. On the other hand, Joe Queenan attacked *Monster's Ball* in the *Guardian* as a "dreary, catatonically paced movie", criticising Forster's "film-school symbolism" and "a wearying mood of claustrophobic self-importance". Summing up, Queenan dismissed *Monster's Ball* as:

…one of those small, earnest, socially conscious movies that audiences are expected – nay, required – to like because its heart is in the right place even if its brain is permanently Awol.

Released in Britain on 7 June 2002, *Monster's Ball* picked up largely favourable reviews, with a few dissenters. Writing in the *Observer*, Philip French compared the film favourably with Hollywood's other recent Death Row dramas: *Dead Man Walking* (1995), *The Last Dance* (1995) and *The Green Mile* (1999). Rating Billy Bob Thornton as "one of the best actors in American cinema", French praised his co-star in less effusive terms: "Halle Berry demonstrates an impressive range of emotions in the best role she's had to date."

Guardian critic Peter Bradshaw felt that the overall film was "an unlikely liberal fantasy", which, ironically, displayed "very conservative racial and sexual politics". He also had mixed feelings about the sex scenes, describing the second coupling as "a very tacky soft-core sequence". Bradshaw had more time for the leads, noting Billy Bob Thornton's "closely observed, unassumingly masculine" performance and praising Halle Berry as "a fiercely intelligent presence". *Monster's Ball* grossed a modest £2 million in the UK, lasting four weeks in the movie top ten.

By the time *Monster's Ball* hit British cinemas, it had acquired a new, Oscar-calibre status. For all the film's merits, it was probably heading for a limited 'arthouse' release before Berry received her Best Actress nomination. The Academy Award nod was merely one in a series of accolades. In 2001, the National Board of Review named Berry as Best Actress for *Monster's Ball*, while the Screen Actors Guild voted her their award for Outstanding Performance by a Female Actor in a Leading Role. On the global scene, the Berlin International Film Festival handed Berry a Silver Bear award for Best Actress. She also picked up Best Actress nominations from the American Film Institute, the Golden Satellite Awards, the Chicago Film Critics Association, the MTV Movie Awards and the Golden Globes.

RIGHT:
A triumphant Halle takes the Best Actress Academy Award for *Monster's Ball*.

Thrilled to be nominated for an Academy Award, Berry claims she didn't seriously expect to win. Interviewed by Louis B Hobson, Berry played down her chances: "I'm trying really hard not to take myself to that whole Oscar thing. It's too overwhelming a thought for me to even comprehend right now." At the same time, Berry couldn't fail to appreciate the significance of her winning. Fifty years earlier, her idol Dorothy Dandridge had come so close: "…the Oscars have eluded black women for so long, so it would be an incredible honour for me."

In fact, a black actress had already won the Academy Award. Six decades earlier, Hattie McDaniel received the Best Supporting Actress Oscar for her

performance in *Gone With the Wind* (1939). Cast as a humble domestic, McDaniel invested her stereotyped character with a certain dignity. Barred from the film's Atlanta premiere, McDaniel harboured few illusions about her place in both Hollywood and society as a whole. Typecast as the movies' favourite 'black mammy', McDaniel played variations on this one role for the rest of her life.

Seven years later, James Baskett portrayed Uncle Remus in Walt Disney's *Song of the South* (1946), a blend of animation and live action. This technically assured yet deeply questionable production is best known for the Oscar-winning song 'Zip a Dee Doo Dah', sung by Baskett. The cast also included Hattie McDaniel, still right at home on a Deep South plantation. Even at the time, the film's crass racial stereotyping drew public protest, led by the National Association for the Advancement of Colored People. Taken aback, Hollywood's film community responded by handing James Baskett a 'special' Academy Award. In fairness, Baskett gives a sincere, good-natured performance, yet his Uncle Remus, a former slave turned loyal servant, is just another variant on Uncle Tom. The Academy's patronising sop to African-Americans did nothing to advance the status of black actors.

Sidney Poitier's emergence as a Hollywood star eventually brought Academy Award recognition. Nominated for *The Defiant Ones* (1958), Poitier took the Best Actor trophy for *Lilies of the Field* (1963). This sentimental, non-confrontational drama cast him as a handyman who helps nuns build a church. Two decades on, Louis Gossett Jr won Best Supporting Actor for playing a rock-hard drill sergeant in *An Officer and a Gentleman*

LEFT:
Halle and Eric
Benet celebrate
her historic Oscar
win at the post-
ceremony party.

(1982). Seven years later, Denzel Washington earned the same award for *Glory* (1989), an American Civil War drama about the first black regiment. In 2002, Washington was nominated Best Actor for the otherwise unremarkable *Training Day* (2001), a tale of police corruption. Washington's rivals for the trophy included fellow black actor Will Smith, nominated for his dynamic performance in the Muhammad Ali biopic, *Ali* (2001).

On 24 March 2002, Berry attended the 74th Annual Academy Awards with husband Eric Benet and mother Judith Berry as her special guests. Aside from her Best Actress nomination, Berry had agreed to present a couple of technical awards, for Best Sound and Best Sound Editing. Berry certainly came dressed for the occasion. Her distinctive 'sheer mesh' Elie Saab outfit included a see-through top embroidered with trailing flowers, artfully covering the crucial areas. The *National Enquirer*'s Style Patrol gave this daring number the thumbs-up: "…worth its weight in gold. Flawless Halle is in a couture class of her own."

Berry had first seen the dress months before the Oscar nominations were announced. Her stylist, Phillip Bloch, brought it along to a Revlon photo shoot. Interviewed by David A Keeps, Berry recalled thinking: "Wow, this is a really great dress but you'd need something wonderful to wear it to." She also felt that the Elie Saab label merited wider exposure: "…and it's nice to feel like you helped somebody out who's so deserving". The original design lacked the heavy-duty decoration, leaving little to the imagination. Given the circumstances, Berry felt it wise to err on the side of modesty: "…we asked for more embroidery and appliques on the upper half to make it less revealing".

When her name was announced as the winner for Best Actress, Berry felt herself losing touch with reality. In a daze, Berry made her way up the steps onto the stage. Struggling to control her emotions, Berry dedicated her award to black women everywhere:

This moment is so much bigger than me. This moment is for Dorothy

Dandridge, Lena Horne, Diahann Carroll. It's for the women that stand beside me – Jada Pinkett, Angela Bassett, Vivica Fox – and it's for every nameless, faceless woman of colour that now has a chance because this door tonight has been opened.

She also thanked her mother Judith, who'd given her so much love and support over the years. While cynics may doubt Berry's insistence that she hadn't written or rehearsed an acceptance speech, her sincerity on the night is beyond question. Berry claims to have little clear memory of her historic win. As she explained to David A Keeps:

> I wasn't even there. I was totally out of my body and don't remember a lot of it … I was just in real disbelief … I was really so elated and I felt the enormity of the moment and it just forced me to leave my body.

Russell Crowe, who'd received a Best Actor nomination for *A Beautiful Mind*, reminded her to keep breathing. Though justifiably proud of her work on *Monster's Ball*, Berry felt the Award represented far more than one outstanding performance by an actress: "It felt bigger than me. It wasn't really so much about me as it was about, hopefully, the changing times."

Looking back on the event, Berry expressed one regret: "I wish I could have been a bit more in control of my emotions … Nobody likes to be that vulnerable and exposed." Berry also felt bad that she'd forgotten to thank *Monster's Ball* writer-director Marc Forster and co-star Billy Bob Thornton. On balance, Berry stands by her acceptance speech, telling *Guardian* journalist Libby Brooks:

> …those things come from my soul, from the reality that I live every day, from the thoughts I think every day. What was in me was what came out of me … I think it's always best to be who you are, and that's who I was in that moment.

That same evening, Denzel Washington won the Best Actor award, while Sidney Poitier received an honorary Lifetime Achievement Oscar. Having partied into the early hours, Berry took both Eric Benet and the Academy Award to bed with her: "My first and only three-way…"

Perhaps inevitably, Berry's Oscar win prompted a certain amount of backlash. Less predictably, it came from the black community. Angela Bassett, who'd turned down the role of Leticia Musgrove, publicly declared that Berry didn't deserve the award. While this attack could be dismissed as an extreme case of sour grapes, it's arguable that Bassett was simply reiterating her original criticism of the character. Sixty years earlier, Hattie McDaniel received her Best Supporting Actress Oscar for playing a 'black mammy' in a Deep South plantation melodrama that depicted slavery in a warm nostalgic glow. Now that Hollywood had finally handed the Best Actress trophy to an African-American, it was for perpetuating a different black stereotype in another tale of Southern lust. Obviously, being mentioned in Berry's Oscar dedication cut no ice with Bassett.

Rising above the criticism, Berry vowed that the Academy Award win would not turn her head. As she explained to David A Keeps: "I think that's what goes wrong with a lot of Oscar winners; they get so picky they pick themselves right out of the game."

AFTER OSCAR

SHORTLY after her Academy Award triumph, Halle Berry was faced with press stories about her father Jerome, now resident in a Cleveland nursing home. Terminally ill with Parkinson's Disease, the 65-year-old Jerome Berry wanted a reconciliation with the daughter he hadn't spoken to for 12 years.

According to tabloid press reports, Berry refused to see him at the Indian Hills Health and Rehabilitation Center in her home town. Renee Berry Graves, Berry's half-sister, announced that Jerome's other children had all forgiven him. Renee also claimed that Jerome Berry had always looked on Halle as his favourite daughter, whatever that meant. Only a cynic would suggest that Berry's hard-won stardom could have anything to do with it. Asked for a comment by the press, Berry made her feelings towards Jerome very clear:

> My father was an alcoholic who abused my mother. I feel like the problems I've had with men have been the result of not having a father all my life.

As if to confirm this, *The National Enquirer* ran another story about Berry's second marriage being in trouble. Just days before Berry's historic win at the Academy Awards, husband Eric Benet supposedly confessed to two extramarital liaisons. Furious that Benet had broken his vow of fidelity, Berry announced that their marriage was over. After Benet begged for forgiveness, she relented and agreed to give him another chance. Understandably wary of her erring

husband, Berry hired a private detective to trail Benet. The reports confirmed her worst suspicions. The *National Enquirer* piece claimed that Benet cheated on Berry with ten other women, including two of her close friends.

Accepting that Benet was suffering from a form of sex addiction, Berry persuaded her husband to seek treatment, having first brandished fresh divorce papers in his face. The *National Enquirer* article even named the clinic where Benet was undergoing therapy: The Meadows, in Wickenburg, Arizona. Reportedly, Benet later admitted to having cheated on Berry just six months into their marriage.

Wary of discussing her troubled relationship, Berry is willing to talk about men's failings in general terms: "...telling the truth works best when dealing with women. They'll never get that." Berry and Benet now appear to be reconciled.

Preoccupied with her personal life, Berry seemed unconcerned when a computer hacker broke into her website, hallewood.com. Having defaced the cartoon Berry with a moustache and beard, the cyberspace vandal sang the praises of white star Nicole Kidman. More worrying, the intruder also mentioned the Ku Klux Klan, America's most notorious racist society. Berry's spokesperson played down the incident: "It sounds very juvenile and child-like."

Months before Berry clutched her Best Actress Academy Award, she had agreed to co-star in MGM/UA's *Die Another Day* (2002), the 20th entry in the official series of James Bond action extravaganzas. Things are heating up

LEFT:
Die Another Day.
Jinx (Halle Berry) shows off her credentials with this homage to *Dr No*.

on the border between North and South Korea. Could it be that some megalomaniac supervillain is attempting to provoke a war in a bid for global domination? Forty years after his first screen assignment, Agent 007 is sent to sort things out.

Cast as the mysterious Jinx, Berry co-starred opposite Bond number five, Irish actor Pierce Brosnan. The producers on *Die Another Day* were Michael G Wilson and Barbara Broccoli, respectively step-son and daughter of series co-founder Albert Broccoli. Their chosen director, New Zealander Lee Tamahori, had made an impressive feature debut with the hard-hitting Maori drama *Once Were Warriors* (1993). Summoned to Hollywood, Tamahori directed the disappointing *Mulholland Falls* (1995), a 1950s crime thriller with Nick Nolte and John Malkovich. Tamahori did better with *The Edge* (1997), a lost-in-Alaska survival drama starring Anthony Hopkins.

Eager to appear in the Bond film, Berry couldn't accept the role of Jinx until she knew the production dates for the *X-Men* sequel. The latter's director, Bryan Singer, wanted to start shooting in early 2002 and *Die Another Day* was scheduled to begin production in January. Contractually bound to reprise her role as Storm in *X-Men 2*, Berry had to wait while Singer and Twentieth Century Fox finalised their deal. The threatened clash was avoided, *X-Men 2* not going before the cameras until June. Free to co-star in *Die Another Day*, Berry received a $4 million (£2.8 million) fee for her role.

The Brosnan Bond era had given the 007 franchise a new lease of life. After the box-office disappointment of *Licence to Kill* (1989), starring Timothy Dalton, the Bond series went on hold for six years. With the exception of *The Long*

Good Friday (1980), few of Pierce Brosnan's pre-Bond films were notable. For a while, it looked like his big screen career had peaked with *The Lawnmower Man* (1992). Three years later, Brosnan became an 'instant' star in *GoldenEye* (1995), ably supported by Judi Dench's 'M' and Samantha Bond's Miss Moneypenny. The film also retained the invaluable services of Desmond Llewelyn's Q, who'd appeared in every official Bond film apart from *Dr No* (1962) and *Live and Let Die* (1973).

Brosnan consolidated his Bond success with *Tomorrow Never Dies* (1997) and *The World is Not Enough* (1999), both major hits. The latter film introduced John Cleese as Q's incoming replacement. This casting proved sadly

BELOW:
Die Another Day.
Halle joins Pierce
Brosnan and the
Aston Martin
Vanquish for the
pre-production
press conference.

84

prescient, as Llewelyn was tragically killed in a car crash shortly after the film's release. Fans unimpressed by Roger Moore's suave lounge lizard regarded Pierce Brosnan as the best Bond since Sean Connery.

The Brosnan-era leading ladies had so far been a mixed bunch. *GoldenEye* featured Izabella Scorupco and future *X-Men* co-star Famke Janssen. *Tomorrow Never Dies* quickly disposed of Teri Hatcher (Lois Lane in TV's *The New Adventures of Superman*) in favour of Hong Kong action star Michelle Yeoh, now famous in the West after *Crouching Tiger, Hidden Dragon* (2000). *The World is Not Enough* contrasted poised French actress Sophie Marceau with fresh-faced American Denise Richards, one of the plucky space cadets in *Starship Troopers* (1997).

The casting of Halle Berry in *Die Another Day* marked a departure of sorts for the series. If nothing else, this was the first Bond movie to pair 007 with an Oscar-winning leading lady; Kim Basinger won her Best Supporting Actress Academy Award, for *LA Confidential*, nearly 15 years after she appeared opposite Sean Connery in *Never Say Never Again*. The latter wasn't an official Bond movie anyway, despite Connery's presence. Unburdened by Oscars, a number of the Bond starlets are today only recalled by diehard fans; even Jane Seymour (*Live and Let Die*) struggled to find another high-profile role before TV's *Dr. Quinn, Medicine Woman* came along. Conversely, both Honor Blackman (*Goldfinger*) and Diana Rigg (*On Her Majesty's Secret Service*) were famous for *The Avengers* when they appeared in Bond films, while Shirley Eaton (*Goldfinger*), Jill St John (*Diamonds Are Forever*) and Britt Ekland (*The Man with the Golden Gun*) all had a healthy number of movie credits.

Bond had become involved with black women in the past, Roger Moore having bedded Gloria Hendry in *Live and Let Die* and Grace Jones in *A View to a Kill*. *Diamonds Are Forever* saw Sean Connery exchanging blows – of the pugilistic kind – with the high-kicking Thumper (Trina Parks), though that doesn't really count.

Asked by David A Keeps why a serious actress would be involved with a Bond movie, Berry gave a straightforward explanation: "You have to balance the art with the commercial projects because it's very much about the business part of it today." Presumably, Dame Judi Dench would give a similar answer. A fan of *Dr No*, the first Bond film she saw, Berry tactfully declined to name her favourite of the series. Nor would she reveal much about her character, Jinx, claiming that "I'm sworn to secrecy. I've signed a paper saying I won't reveal anything." That said, most press reports on the film referred to Jinx as a villain. The title remained more of a mystery, with Bond number 20 initially referred to as 'Beyond the Ice'.

It's rumoured that *Die Another Day*'s early script drafts reunited Brosnan's Bond with Wai Lin, Michelle Yeoh's kung fu fighting Chinese agent from *Tomorrow Never Dies*. When it became clear that the busy Yeoh couldn't make the filming dates, her character fell by the wayside. To fill the gap, Berry's role was rewritten and expanded.

The film also featured a dual contribution from hard-wearing pop icon Madonna. Having agreed to provide the movie's theme song, she also accepted a bit part as a fencing instructor. Despite an extensive filmography, Madonna has never really cut it as a movie star. Between the big screen highs – relatively speaking – of

Desperately Seeking Susan (1985) and *Evita* (1996), there were the mega-turkeys *Shanghai Surprise* (1986), *Who's That Girl?* (1987) and *Body of Evidence* (1992). A competent supporting player in movies such as *Dick Tracy* (1990) and *A League of Their Own* (1992), Madonna seems more comfortable as a co-star.

When Madonna's name was first linked to *Die Another Day*, it was rumoured that her involvement with the secret agent spoof *Austin Powers: The Spy Who Shagged Me* (1999) would deter the Bond producers. Disappointed that her character didn't get intimate with 007, Madonna requested a script rewrite, turning her into a lesbian. Despite the ensuing publicity, this was not really a first for the series. While *Goldfinger* had toned down the Sapphic leanings of Ian Fleming's Pussy Galore, she nevertheless spent a lot of time hanging with her all-girl flying stunt team. And, before even that, Lotte Lenya's Rosa Klebb in *From Russia With Love* was certainly a lot more interested in Daniela Bianchi than Sean Connery.

Berry's work on *Die Another Day* lasted four months. Production on the film began on 14 January 2002, the exotic international locations embracing Iceland, Hawaii, Spain and Cornwall's Eden Project. Most of the film's interiors were shot at Pinewood Studios, just outside London. During production in England, Berry discovered a taste for afternoon tea with scones and clotted cream. Between takes, however, she exercised in her trailer, keeping those all-important stomach muscles in shape. Back in LA, she had done regular weight training, though not enough to harden her "soft and womanly" figure.

Berry got on well with leading man Pierce Brosnan. Significantly, she praised Brosnan's commitment to his wife and sons, telling David A Keeps: "…it's great because he's such a family man and I like to see a man putting the needs of his family first." Commenting on Brosnan's fourth outing as 007, Berry echoed the sentiments of most fans: "As far as being Bond, he wears it well." Brosnan is well known for his dislike of shooting sex scenes, even with a co-star like Halle Berry. Fortunately for the Bond image, this antipathy is never evident in the finished films, a tribute to Brosnan's acting ability.

In March, Berry took a break from the Bond shoot to attend the Academy Awards ceremony back in Los Angeles. Just 48 hours after her Oscar win and highly emotional acceptance speech, Berry returned to the *Die Another Day* set, putting in 14-hour days.

Berry suffered a potentially serious accident during the shoot in Cadiz, Spain (standing in for Cuba, Havana). Filming a stunt scene involving a helicopter on 10 April, she was injured by a smoke grenade blast, which left a fragment of casing lodged in her left eye. Rushed to hospital, Berry underwent a 30-minute operation. Left with a sore and very swollen eye, the star escaped any permanent damage. For his part, Brosnan had to take time off during the British leg of the production when both his sons were taken ill in quick succession.

Die Another Day received its world premiere on 18 November. Chosen for the annual Royal Film Performance, the movie was screened at the Royal Albert Hall in the presence of Queen Elizabeth II and Prince Philip. On Her Majesty's Secret Service indeed. The money raised by this charity premiere went to the Cinema and Television Benevolent Fund. Sold with the tagline 'He's Never Been Cooler', *Die Another Day* then

ABOVE:
Die Another Day.
Halle and Pierce
Brosnan on location
in Cadiz, Spain,
in April 2002.

went on general release in both Britain and the United States four days later, on 22 November.

"Realizing the [Bond] franchise is challenged by youth movies like *XXX*," opined Kirk Honeycutt in *The Hollywood Reporter*, "the Bond producers raise the ante so James stays reasonably hip. Madonna sings the title song and even appears in one of the film's brighter sequences. This also is the first Bond film to rely heavily on digital effects. But the best addition is Halle Berry, who instead of being a Bond Girl du jour, joins forces with 007 as a full-fledged fighting companion, matching him in ruthlessness and

technology … That Brosnan and Berry have so little opportunity to develop their characters and relationship with each other is a shame. But the international market probably doesn't understand the double-entendres anyway."

Other critics were less convinced of Berry's suitability for the role. In the *Chicago Tribune*, Mark Caro pointed out that "Berry, no surprise, looks great, but her presence contributes more to the marketing than the story. She also doesn't seem comfortable delivering such lame lines as, 'Switch [the laser] off or I'm going to be half the girl I used to be.'"

Ray Greene, meanwhile, noted in *Boxoffice Magazine* that "when Halle Berry rises like Venus from the surf, she's ... wearing a knock-off of Ursula Andress' bikini from [the] first cinematic Bond adventure. Halle looks wrong in Ursula's outfit, actually, and wrong for the Bond world. The Bond aesthetic of feminine beauty is determinedly pre-feminist, epitomized by Amazonian impossibilities like Andress and Jill St John, and by British agent Miranda Frost (Rosamund Pike) here. Berry's beauty is a bit too delicate, a bit too *Vogue* and not *Playboy* enough, to make a satisfactory Bond girl, and Tamahori's flat and conventional directing style does little to mask the fact that this supposed superwoman runs, well, like a girl, and shoots a gun like she's worried she may break a nail."

With barely time for a costume change, Berry then reported for superhero duty on *X-Men 2*. When a mutant attempts to assassinate the President of the United States, things become even tougher for Professor Xavier's band of superheroes. While they saved the world at the end of the first film, mutants are still regarded with fear and hatred. Berry reprised her role as Storm, or Ororo Munroe, alongside original co-stars Patrick Stewart, Ian McKellen, Hugh Jackman, Anna Paquin, Famke Janssen and James Marsden. Shaun Ashmore returned as Iceman, briefly seen as a young student in *X-Men*, while British actor Alan Cumming signed up to play new X-Men recruit Nightcrawler. In the comic book, Nightcrawler is a humorous, blue-faced imp with the power of teleportation. Having triumphed on stage as the high-camp MC in *Cabaret*, Cumming seemed ideal casting.

Alongside Magneto, the producers decided to try a new super villain, so Scottish actor Brian Cox came on board as Stryker. Cox is the original, and some say the best, screen incarnation of Hannibal Lecter, having played the character in *Manhunter* (1986). His other American credits include *Rob Roy* (1994), *Braveheart* (1995), *The Long Kiss Goodnight* (1996) and *Rushmore* (1998). The role of Lady Deathstrike, Stryker's partner in supercrime, went to Chinese-American star Kelly Hu. After a decade of often thankless roles in movies like *Harley Davidson and the Marlboro Man* (1991) and *Surf Ninjas* (1993), Hu attracted attention in *The Scorpion King* (2002), playing opposite wrestling star The Rock.

Production on *X-Men 2* started on 3 June 2002, with location shooting in Vancouver, Canada, subsequently moving to Detroit and New York City. During a break in her schedule, Berry and her stepdaughter India supposedly travelled to Arizona, where estranged husband Eric Benet was undergoing sex addiction treatment at The Meadows clinic. *X-Men 2* was released in the United States on 2 May 2 2003, opening in Britain a day earlier.

Pleased with Berry's work on *Die Another Day*, not to mention her Academy Award triumph, MGM/UA offered the star a two-film deal reportedly worth $12 million. First up is a remake of *Foxy Brown* (1974), which Berry will also co-produce. This blaxploitation favourite starred Pam Grier, a tough act to follow. MGM had already produced a remake of *Shaft* (2001), casting Samuel L Jackson as Richard Roundtree's nephew.

In the original *Foxy Brown*, Pam Grier played a nurse who wages war on a gang of drug dealers. Aside from their evil dope-peddling, the latter murdered

Foxy's lover, an undercover narcotics cop. Having slashed and burned her way through most of the bad guys, Foxy castrates one villain and sends the pickled genitalia to his girlfriend, the gang's leader. Don't expect to see this memorable payoff recreated in the new version.

In truth, *Foxy Brown* is markedly inferior to Pam Grier's earlier *Coffy* (1973), yet the catchy title has assumed an iconic life of its own. Quentin Tarantino's *Jackie Brown* (1997), also starring Grier, is an obvious homage. Mike Myers' third Austin Powers movie, *Austin Powers in Goldmember* (2002), features a character called Foxy Cleopatra, a double tribute to *Foxy Brown* and the lesser-known *Cleopatra Jones* (1973).

Interviewed in *Variety*, MGM spokesman Alex Gartner outlined the studio's new, post-millennial vision of the character: "We're going to take all the positive aspects of Foxy, as a powerful, empowered woman, and we're going to create a larger-than-life vehicle for Halle."

The second project in Halle Berry's MGM/UA deal is *Brown-Eyed Girl*. In development for a number of years, the script deals with a modern woman's search for romance. Furthermore, Berry's success as Jinx in *Die Another Day* has interested the studio in creating a spinoff movie around the character, though not without a warning note from *Boxoffice Magazine*: "If the Bond producers are serious about spinning this character off, it probably has more to do with the success of knock-offs like *Scorpion King* (which launched the Rock, like bright-eyed Athena from the brow of Zeus, out of the Brendan Fraser *Mummy* films) than it does Berry's inherent rightness in the part."

Berry is also set to star in *Need*, loosely based on a novel by Lawrence David. Berry will play a high-flying New York psychotherapist who discovers that her husband is having an affair. Even worse, his lover is one of her own patients, a neurotic young woman with a self-destructive streak. The latter will probably be played by Marisa Tomei.

Then there's the *Bridget Jones*-style romantic comedy *Nappily Ever After*, adapted from a book by Trisha Thomas. Co-producer Berry will play Venus, an advertising executive who splits from her long-term boyfriend, tired of waiting for him to pop the question. When he rapidly becomes involved in a new romance, she begins to have second thoughts.

The harrowing drama *October Squall* is a return to *Monster's Ball* territory. Berry is cast as a pregnant rape victim who decides to keep her baby son. When the child hits adolescence, she becomes afraid that he's inherited his father's violent tendencies. Berry has also agreed to reunite with producer Joel Silver for the horror movie *Gothika*. Berry will play a criminal psychologist who wakes up in a mental hospital, accused of a murder she can't remember. The film is set to co-star Robert Downey Jr and Spanish actress Penélope Cruz.

Berry also plans to work with Oprah Winfrey on another deluxe TV movie. Produced by Winfrey's company for the ABC network, *Their Eyes Were Watching* is based on a 1937 novel by Neale Hurston. While Winfrey's earlier *The Wedding* doesn't count among Berry's career highpoints, this new project offers a challenging dramatic role.

On top of all this, Warner Bros has offered Berry the title role in their longstanding *Catwoman* project, a

LEFT:
February 2003.
Halle attends the
Italian premiere of
Die Another Day.

RIGHT:
Halle with Eric
Benet at the 2002
National Board of
Review Awards,
held in New York.

spinoff from the studio's patchy *Batman* series. Michelle Pfeiffer played the character in Tim Burton's perverse-yet-gloomy *Batman Returns* (1992). The high-camp 1960s television *Batman* got through three Catwomen, including black cabaret artiste Eartha Kitt, who worked with Berry on *Boomerang*.

Berry's rocky marriage to Eric Benet continues to provoke press speculation. In December 2002, the *National Enquirer* reported that Berry was putting her film career on hold to start a family. According to the article, Berry believed that having a child with Benet would strengthen their relationship. Berry was quoted as saying: "It has been a great year and now I want to get pregnant."

While Berry still feels that she fights racism "every day", things seem to be getting better. Interviewed by Louis B Hobson, Berry expressed guarded optimism: "I think the business is less colour blind, but ... it's still a struggle for some directors to believe it's OK to cast me in everything." Discussing her Oscar success with David A Keeps, Berry explained: "I hope I'm on my way to being just Halle Berry, the actress, not always being black first."

As an Academy Award winner, 007 star and eco-friendly superhero, she stands more than a chance. Halle Berry has certainly come a long way since shaking her booty in *The Last Boy Scout*:

I've gotten some great offers to work with really good directors and really good scripts for parts that are not written specifically for a black woman. That shows something is changing ... It feels really good to be in that category; it's my dream that it will continue. Not only for me, but for other women of colour.

FILMOGRAPHY

1991

JUNGLE FEVER
Universal/Forty Acres and a Mule Filmworks
132 mins

Producer: Spike Lee; Director: Spike Lee; Screenplay: Spike Lee; Director of photography: Ernest Dickerson; Production design: Wynn Thomas; Editing: Sam Pollard, Brunilda Torres; Music: Terence Blanchard, Stevie Wonder.

Cast: Wesley Snipes (Flipper Purify), Annabella Sciorra (Angie), Spike Lee (Cyrus), Ossie Davis (the Good Reverend Doctor Purify), Ruby Dee (Lucinda Purify), Samuel L Jackson (Gator Purify), Lonette McKee (Drew), John Turturro (Paulie Carbone), Anthony Quinn (Lou Carbone), Tim Robbins (Jerry), Brad Dourif (Leslie), Halle Berry (Vivian).

STRICTLY BUSINESS
Warner/Island World
83 mins

Producers: Pam Gibson, Andre Harrell; Associate producer: Nelson George; Directors: Kevin Hooks, Rolando Hudson [uncredited]; Screenplay: Nelson George, Pam Gibson; Director of photography: Zoltan David; Production design: Ruth Ammon; Editing: Richard Nord; Music: Michel Colombier.

Cast: Tommy Davidson (Bobby Johnson), Joseph C. Phillips (Waymon Tinsdale III), Anne Marie Johnson (Diedre), David Marshall Grant (David), Halle Berry (Natalie), Jon Cypher (Drake), Samuel L Jackson (Monroe), Kim Coles (Millicent).

THE LAST BOY SCOUT
Warner/Geffen/Silver
105 mins

Producers: Joel Silver, Michael Levy; Director: Tony Scott; Screenplay: Shane Black; Director of photography: Ward Russell; Production design: Brian Morris; Editing: Stuart Baird, Mark Goldblatt, Mark Helfrich; Music: Michael Kamen.

Cast: Bruce Willis (Joe Hallenbeck), Damon Wayans (Jimmy Dix), Chelsea Field (Sarah Hallenbeck), Noble Willingham (Sheldon Marcone), Taylor Negron (Milo), Halle Berry (Cory), Bruce McGill (Mike Matthews), Danielle Harris (Darian Hallenbeck), Chelcie Ross (Senator Baynard), Joe Santis (Bessalo).

1992

BOOMERANG
Paramount
117 mins

Producers: Brain Grazer, Warrington Hudlin; Director: Reginald Hudlin; Screenplay: Barry W Blaustein, David Sheffield; Director of photography: Woody Omens; Production design: Jane Musky; Editing: Earl Watson, John Carter, Michael Jablow; Music: Marcus Miller.

Cast: Eddie Murphy (Marcus Graham), Robin Givens (Jacqueline Broyer), Halle Berry (Angela Lewis), David Alan Grier (Gerard Jackson), Martin Lawrence (Tyler), Grace Jones (Strange), Geoffrey Holder (Nelson), Eartha Kitt (Lady Eloise), Melvin Van Peebles (editor).

1993

QUEEN
aka *ALEX HALEY'S QUEEN*
CBS [TVM]
tx 14 February

Producer: Bernard Sofronski; Director: John Erman; Screenplay: David Stevens (from a story by Alex Haley); Editing: James Galloway, Paul LaMastra.

Cast: Halle Berry (Queen), Ann-Margret (Sally Jackson), Ossie Davis (Parson Dick), Danny Glover (Alec Haley), Lonette McKee (Alice), Martin Sheen (James Jackson Sr), Paul Winfield (Cap'n Jack), Dennis Haysbert (Davis).

CB4
Universal
89 mins

Producer: Nelson George, Director: Tamra Davis; Screenplay: Chris Rock, Nelson George, Robert LoCash; Director of photography: Karl Walter Lindenlaub; Production design: Nelson Coates; Editing: Earl Watson; Music: John Barnes.

Cast: Chris Rock (Albert), Allen Payne (Euripides), Deezer D (Otis), Phil Hartman (Virgil Robinson), Theresa Randle (Eve), Charlie Murphy (Gusto), Ice T (himself), Ice Cube (himself), Flavour Flav (himself). Halle Berry (herself)

FATHER HOOD
Buena Vista / Hollywood
94 mins

Producers: Nicholas Pileggi, Anant Singh, Gillian Gorfil;
Director: Darrell James Roodt, Screenplay: Scott Spencer;
Director of photography: Mark Vicente; Production design:
David Barkham; Music: Patrick O'Hearn.

Cast: Patrick Swayze (Jack Charles), Halle Berry (Kathleen
Mercer), Diane Ladd (Rita), Brian Bonsall (Eddie Charles),
Sabrina Lloyd (Kelly Charles), Michael Ironside (Jerry),
Bob Gunton (Lazzaro).

THE PROGRAM
Touchstone / Samuel Goldwyn / Buena Vista
114 mins

Producer: Samuel Goldwyn Jr; Director: David S Ward;
Screenplay: David S Ward, Aaron Latham; Director of
photography: Victor Hammer, Production design: Albert
Brenner; Editing: Paul Seydor, Kimberly Ray; Music:
Michel Colombier.

Cast: James Caan (Coach Winters), Halle Berry (Autumn
Haley), Omar Epps (Darnell Jefferson), Craig Sheffer
(Joe Kane), Kristy Swanson (Camille), Abraham Benrubi
(Bud-Lite Kaminski), Duane Davis (Alvin Mack).

1994

THE FLINTSTONES
Universal / Amblin / Hanna-Barbera
92 mins

Producer: Bruce Cohen; Director: Brian Levant; Screenplay:
Tom S Parker, Jim Jennewein, Steven E De Souza [and many
others, uncredited]; Director of photography: Dean Cundey;
Production design: William Sandell; Editing: Kent Beyda;
Music: David Newman.

Cast: John Goodman (Fred Flintstone), Rick Moranis (Barney
Rubble), Elizabeth Perkins (Wilma Flintstone), Rosie O'Donnell
(Betty Rubble), Elizabeth Taylor (Pearl Slaghoople), Kyle
MacLachlan (Cliff Vandercave), Halle Berry (Sharon Stone),
Jonathan Winters (grizzled man).

1995

SOLOMON AND SHEBA
Showtime Networks [TVM]
tx 26 February

Producers: Dino DeLaurentiis, Martha Schumacher; Director:
Robert M Young; Screenplay: Ronnie Kern; Director of
photography: Giuseppe Maccari; Production design: Pier Luigi
Basile; Editing: Arthur Coburn; Music: David Kitay.

Cast: Halle Berry (Nikhaule / Sheba), Jimmy Smits (Solomon),
Kenneth Colley (Nathan), Nickolas Grace (Jeroboam), Hugh
Quarshie (Nikhaule's father), Miquel Brown (housekeeper),
Nadia Sawalha (first prostitute), Laura Fuino (second
prostitute), Sergio Smacchi (Hadad).

LOSING ISAIAH
Paramount
106 mins

Producers: Howard W. Koch Jnr., Naomi Foner; Director:
Stephen Gyllenhaal; Screenplay: Naomi Foner (based on the
novel by Seth Margolis); Director of photography: Andrzej
Bartowiak; Production design: Jeannine C Oppewall; Editing:
Harvey Rosenstock; Music: Mark Isham.

Cast: Jessica Lange (Margaret Lewin), Halle Berry (Khaila
Richards), David Straithairn (Charles Lewin), Cuba Gooding
Jnr. (Eddie Hughes), Samuel L. Jackson (Kadar Lewis), Marc
John Jeffries (Isaiah).

1996

EXECUTIVE DECISION
aka *CRITICAL DECISION*
Warner / Silver Pictures
132 mins

Producers: Joel Silver, Jim Thomas, John Thomas; Director:
Stuart Baird; Screenplay: Jim Thomas, John Thomas; Director
of photography: Alex Thomson; Production design: Terence
Marsh; Editing: Dallas Puett, Frank J Urioste, Stuart Baird,
Kevin Stitt, Derek Brechin; Music: Jerry Goldsmith.

Cast: Kurt Russell (David Grant), Halle Berry (Jean), John

Leguizamo (Rat), Steven Seagal (Lieutenant Colonel Austin Travis), Oliver Platt (Dennis Cahill), Joe Morton (Cappy), David Suchet (Nagi Hassan), B D Wong (Louie), Len Cariou (Charles White), Whip Hubley (Baker), J T Walsh (Senator Mavros).

RACE THE SUN
Columbia TriStar
82 mins

Producers: Richard Heus, Barry Morrow; Director: Charles T Kanganis; Screenplay: Barry Morrow; Director of photography: David Burr; Production design: Owen Patterson; Editing: Wendy Greene Beaumont; Music: Graeme Revell. Halle Berry (Miss Sandra Beecher), Casey Affleck (Daniel Webster), Eliza Dushku (Cindy Johnson), Sara Tanaka (Uni Kakamura), Bill Hunter (Commissioner Hawkes), James Belushi (Frank Machi).

GIRL 6
TCF/Fox-Searchlight/40 Acres and a Mule
108 mins

Producer: Spike Lee; Director: Spike Lee; Screenplay: Suzan-Lori Parks; Director of photography: Malik Hassan Sayeed; Production design: Ina Mayhew; Editing: Sam Pollard; Music: Prince.
Cast: Theresa Randle (Girl 6), Isaiah Washington (Shoplifter), Spike Lee (Jimmy), Jenifer Lewis (Boss 1), Debi Mazar (Girl 39), Peter Berg (Caller 1), Michael Imperioli (Scary Caller 30), Naomi Campbell (Girl 75), Quentin Tarantino (Q.T.), Madonna (Boss 3), John Turturro (Murray the agent), Ron Silver (Director 2, LA), Halle Berry (herself).

THE RICH MAN'S WIFE
Buena Vista/Hollywood/Caravan
94 mins

Producers: Roger Birnbaum, Julie Bergman Sender; Director: Amy Holden Jones; Screenplay: Amy Holden Jones; Director of photography: Haskell Wexler; Production design: Jeannine Oppewall; Editing: Wendy Greene Bricmont; Music: John Frizzell, James Newton Howard.

Cast: Halle Berry (Josie Potenza), Christopher McDonald (Tony Potenza), Clive Owen (Jake Golden), Peter Greene (Cole Wilson), Charles Hallahan (Detective Dan Fredricks), Frankie Faison (Detective Ron Lewis), Clea Lewis (Nora Golden).

1997
B.A.P.S.
New Line/Island
92 mins

Producers: Mark Burg, Loretha Jones; Director: Robert Townsend; Screenplay: Troy Beyer; Director of photography: Bill Dill; Production design: Keith Brian Burns; Editing: Patrick Kennedy; Music: Stanley Clarke.

Cast: Halle Berry (Nisi), Martin Landau (Mr Blakemore), Ian Richardson (Manley), Natalie Desselle (Mickey), Troy Beyer (Tracy), Luigi Amodeo (Antonio), Jonathan Fried (Isaac).

1998
THE WEDDING
aka OPRAH WINFREY PRESENTS: THE WEDDING
Harpo Films [TVM]
tx 22 February 1998

Producer: Doro Bachrach; Director: Charles Burnett; Screenplay: Lisa Jones (from the novel by Dorothy West); Director of photography: Frederick Elmes; Production design: Geoffrey S Grimsman; Editing: Dorian Harris; Music: Stephen James Taylor.

Cast: Halle Berry (Shelby Coles), Eric Thal (Meade Howell), Lynne Whitfield (Corinne Coles), Carl Lumbly (Lute), Michael Warren (Clark Coles), Shirley Knight (Gram), Cynda Williams (Liz).

BULWORTH
Twentieth Century Fox
108 mins

Executive producer: Lauren Shuler Donner; Producers: Warren Beatty, Pieter Jan Brugge; Co-producers: Victoria Thomas, Frank Capra III; Director: Warren Beatty; Screenplay: Warren Beatty, Jeremy Pikser and [uncredited] James Toback, Aaron Sorkin; Director of photography: Vittorio Storaro; Production design: Dean Tavoularis; Editing: Robert C Jones, Billy Weber; Original music: Ennio Morricone.

Cast: Warren Beatty (Jay Billington Bulworth), Halle Berry (Nina), Don Cheadle (LD), Oliver Platt (Dennis Murphy), Paul Sorvino (Graham Crockett), Jack Warden (Eddie Davers), Isaiah Washington (Darnell).

WHY DO FOOLS FALL IN LOVE
Warner Bros / Rhino Films
116 mins

Executive producer: Gregory Nava; Producers: Paul Hall,
Steve Nemeth; Director: Gregory Nava; Screenplay: Tina
Andrews; Director of photography: Ed Lachman; Production
design: Cary White; Editing: Nancy Richardson; Music:
Stephen James Taylor.

Cast: Halle Berry (Zola Taylor), Larenz Tate (Frankie Lymon),
Vivica A Fox (Elizabeth 'Mickey' Waters), Lela Rochon (Emira
Eagle), Little Richard (himself).

WELCOME TO HOLLYWOOD
Blump International Films / Crystal Spring
Productions / Filmsmith Productions / Stone Canyon
Entertainment
89 mins
Producer: Zachary Matz; Directors: Tony Markes, Adam
Rifkin; Screenplay: Tony Markes, Adam Rifkin; Director of
photography: Kramer Morgenthau; Editing: Joy Zimmerman;
Music: Justin Reinhardt.

Cast: Tony Markes (Anton Markwell aka Nick Decker),
Adam Rifkin (himself), Halle Berry (herself).

1999
INTRODUCING DOROTHY DANDRIDGE
aka *FACE OF AN ANGEL*
Home Box Office [TVM]
tx 14 August

Producer: Larry Y Albucher; Director: Martha Coolidge;
Screenplay: Shonda Rhimes (from the book by Earl Mills);
Director of photography: Robbie Greenberg; Production
design: James Spencer; Editing: Alan Heim; Music:
Elmer Bernstein.

Cast: Halle Berry (Dorothy Dandridge), Brent Spiner
(Earl Mills), Klaus Maria Brandauer (Otto Preminger),
Obba Babatunde (Harold Nicholas), Loretta Devine
(Ruby Dandridge), Cynda Williams (Vivian Dandridge),
LaTanya Richardson (Auntie), Tamara Taylor (Geri Nicholas),
D B Sweeney (Jack Denison), William Atherton (Darryl F Zanuck).

2000
X-MEN
Twentieth Century Fox / Donner-Schuler Donner
Productions / Marvel Entertainment
104 mins

Producers: Lauren Schuler Donner, Ralph Winter; Director:
Bryan Singer; Screenplay: David Hayter (based on a story by
Bryan Singer and Tom De Santo); Director of photography:
Newton Thomas Sigel; Production design: John Myhre;
Editing: Steven Rosenblum, Kevin Stitt, John Wright; Music:
Michael Kamen, Jeremy Sweet.

Cast: Patrick Stewart (Professor Charles Xavier), Ian McKellen
(Erik Magnus Lehnsherr / Magneto), Hugh Jackman
(Logan / Wolverine), Halle Berry (Ororo Munroe / Storm),
Famke Janssen (Jean Grey), James Marsden (Scott
Summers / Cyclops), Anna Paquin (Marie D'Ancanto / Rogue),
Bruce Davison (Senator Robert Kelly), Tyler Mane (Sabretooth),
Ray Park (Toad), Rebecca Romijn-Stamos (Mystique).

2001
SWORDFISH
Warner / Silver Pictures / Jonathan Krane Group
99 mins

Producers: Jonathan Krane, Joel Silver, Paul Winze;
Director: Dominic Sena; Screenplay: Skip Woods; Director of
photography: Paul Cameron; Production design: Jeff Mann;
Editing: Stephen E Rivkin; Music: Paul Oakenfold,
Christopher Young.

Cast: John Travolta (Gabriel Shear), Hugh Jackman
(Stanley Jobson), Halle Berry (Ginger Knowles),
Don Cheadle (Agent Roberts), Vinnie Jones (Marco),
Sam Shepard (Reisman), Camryn Grimes (Holly).

MONSTER'S BALL
Lions Gate Films / Lee Daniels Entertainment
111 mins

Producer: Lee Daniels; Director: Marc Forster; Screenplay:
Milo Addica, Will Rokos and Marc Forster [uncredited];
Director of photography: Roberto Schaefer; Production design:
Monroe Kelly; Editing: Matt Chesse; Music: Chris Beaty,
Thad Spencer, Richard Werbowenko.

Cast: Halle Berry (Leticia Musgrove), Billy Bob Thornton
(Hank Grotowski), Peter Boyle (Buck Grotowski), Heath
Ledger (Sonny Grotowski), Sean Combs (Lawrence Musgrove),
Coronji Calhoun (Tyrell Musgrove).

2002
DIE ANOTHER DAY
Metro-Goldwyn-Mayer / United Artists / Eon
Productions / Danjaq Productions
132 mins

Producers: Barbara Broccoli, Michael G Wilson; Director: Lee Tamahori; Screenplay: Neal Purvis, Robert Wade; Director of photography: David Tattersall; Production design: Peter Lamont; Editing: Christian Wagner; Music: David Arnold. Cast: Pierce Brosnan (James Bond), Halle Berry (Jinx), Toby Stephens (Gustav Graves), Rick Yune (Zao), Rosamund Pike (Miranda Frost), Michael Madsen (Damian Falco), Judi Dench (M), Samantha Bond (Miss Moneypenny), John Cleese (Q).

2003

X2: X-MEN UNITED
Twentieth Century Fox/Donner-Schuler Donner/Marvel Entertainment
135 mins

Producers: Lauren Schuler Donner, Ralph Winter; Director: Bryan Singer; Screenplay: David Hayter, Bryan Singer, Michael Dougherty, Daniel P Harris, Zak Penn; Director of photography: Newton Thomas Sigel; Production design: Guy Dyas; Music: John Ottman.

Cast: Patrick Stewart (Professor Xavier), Ian McKellen (Erik Magnus Lehnsherr/Magneto), Brian Cox (Stryker), Halle Berry (Ororo Munroe/Storm), Hugh Jackman (Logan/Wolverine), Famke Janssen (Jean Grey), James Marsden (Scott Summers/Cyclops), Anna Paquin (Marie D'Ancanto/Rogue), Alan Cumming (Nightcrawler), Kelly Hu (Lady Deathstrike), Rebecca Romijn-Stamos (Mystique), Shaun Ashmore (Iceman), Aaron Stanford (Pyro), Katie Stuart (Kitty Pride).

Television credits
(excepting those mentioned in main text)
1995
Mad TV (herself)
1998
AFI's 100 Years...100 Movies
1999
The Kennedy Center Honors
The 51st Annual Primetime Emmy Awards
2000
31st NAACP Image Awards
MTV Movie Awards
2001
32nd NAACP Image Awards
73rd Annual Academy Awards
America: A Tribute to Heroes
Concert for New York City
The Making of 'Swordfish'
2002
The Orange British Academy Film Awards
Leute heute
Seitenblicke
The Bernie Mac Show – 'Handle Your Business' (herself)

BIBLIOGRAPHY

Brooks, Libby. 'Now I'm really at the party.' *The Guardian*, Thursday 6 June 2002.

Frischauer, Willi. *Behind the Scenes of Otto Preminger*, Michael Joseph (London) 1973.

Goring, Rosemary (ed). *Larousse Dictionary of Writers*, Larousse (Edinburgh) 1994.

Hobson, Louis B. 'Ball rolling for Halle', *Calgary Sun*, Saturday 9 February 2002.
'Berry, Berry happy'. *Calgary Sun*, Monday 7 January 2002.

Kirkland, Bruce. 'Berry denies extra pay to bare breasts', *Toronto Sun*, Monday 4 June 2001.
'Black And White In Color', *Toronto Sun*, 12 March 1995.

McLeod, Tyler, 'Halle's no fool', *Calgary Sun*, Saturday 22 August 1998.

Parish, James Robert, *The Hollywood Book of Death*, Contemporary Books (New York) 2002.

Pym, John (ed). *Time Out Film Guide, Ninth Edition*, Penguin (London) 2000.

Queenan, Joe, 'Dropping the ball', *The Guardian*, Saturday 8 June 2002.

Reynolds, Richard, *Super Heroes*, Batsford (London), 1992.

Ross, Jonathan, *The Incredibly Strange Film Book*, Simon & Schuster (London) 1993.

Taylor, Robin, 'Belle of the Ball', *The Southern Daily Echo*, Friday 7 June 2002.

Thompson, Bob, 'Minding her X's and O's', *Toronto Sun*, Wednesday 12 July 2000.
'She's a fool for love', *Toronto Sun*, Sunday 30 August 1998.

Walker, John, *Halliwell's Film & Video Guide 2001*, HarperCollins (London) 2000.

Halliwell's Filmgoer's Companion, 10th Edition, HarperCollins (London) 1993.